Wooden toys that work

In gratitude to Ita Bay, Angus McKinnon,
and Robert Vinestock whose help and
encouragement in my Toymaking have led to
the writing of this book.

Wooden toys that work

Marion Cathcart Millett
Creator of Whim-Wham Toys

Diagrams by Roy Mole, after
the author's sketches

Mills & Boon Limited London

First published in Great Britain 1974
by Mills & Boon Limited, 17–19 Foley Street,
London, W1A 1DR.

© Marion Cathcart Millett 1974

ISBN 0.263.05432.2

Cover photograph by courtesy of
Francis Canning, Edinburgh

Made and printed in Great Britain by
Butler & Tanner Ltd, Frome and London.

Contents

Introduction

Many people all over the world like to make things with their hands. Still more people would like to do so if they only knew how. Often lack of opportunity makes them doubt their ability and prevents them from trying. Consequently they tend to sigh with envy and frustration at the skill of others, while if they only knew, they could develop skills for themselves, which carry their own reward in self-expression and in the joy of creation.

This book is designed for people who (like the author) have had no formal training in woodwork. They may be quite young or they may have reached the age of fifty or sixty (again like the author) without having handled any tools other than a hammer or a screw-driver. In addition, they may find the usual woodworkers' drawings too difficult to follow. This book can also help people who have skill in woodwork but have not thought of using it to make toys, or who do not know how to set about it.

The first chapter is therefore devoted to the necessary tools and equipment, the second chapter is an introduction to the application of colour in a harmonious way—a fascinating study in itself. In the following pages are patterns which can be transferred directly to the wood itself—a unique feature of this book, which should enable anyone to try his or her hand at making these toys for themselves. Toys which have, for the most part, a magical quality of movement and are much beloved by children.

I should mention, perhaps, that although it is only within the last years that I have taken to toy-making seriously, my first attempt to make movable wooden toys happened more than thirty years ago when my children were small. At that time I first experienced the practical, pedagogical ideas of the Austrian educator and philosopher, Rudolf Steiner (1861–1925) and attempted to apply them in starting a Nursery School on his lines in the Surrey village where we were then living. It was wartime and we were fortunate to discover a semi-retired lady, trained in his methods, who was happy to escape from London and to help us.

Now we learnt that Dr. Steiner indicated that it is very important for small children to have movable toys, toys they can manipulate to produce an effect. However, since it was wartime, the only way we could get such toys was to make them ourselves; and a group of interested parents did just this. Waterfalls, acrobats, men that hammer, men that saw, and similar toys, we somehow managed to contrive, to the delight and enrichment of the children. Time went on, the children grew older, the war came to an end, and the Nursery Class and our need for toys came to an end also.

The need, as far as I was concerned, did not arise again until six years ago, when I was asked to help raise funds for a Church Bazaar in Edinburgh, where I now live. I recognised that the need for this kind of toy is even greater now than thirty years ago; for today, far too many unsuitable, even dangerous toys, which can do more harm than good to children, are all too easily obtainable.

Dr. Steiner stressed how important it is for children to have scope for their imagination, and to have beauty in the things they handle during their formative years. All too many modern toys have just the reverse effect, as more and more people realise today. The demand and need for creative toymaking has never been greater than now. This is why I should like to invite other people to share in this most pleasurable of pursuits.

The designs of the toys have been very carefully worked out and tested and they should be copied with the utmost exactitude at first. Improvisations and improvements can follow later, but it must be emphasised that the exact positioning of drill holes and distances is essential for success. Although previous skill and experience are not required to make these toys, accuracy is all-important and must be achieved, or the results will be disappointing.

Skill and precision grow with practice, giving great joy as they develop. Working in wood is a most fascinating and absorbing activity. "Sorrows flee away!" One's eyes are opened to new worlds revealed in the textures and grains of the various woods. Pine, beech, teak, birch—how different they all look and feel! New ideas come as one works, an odd-shaped piece of wood will suggest a new toy: one finds oneself becoming more resourceful and capable, not only in craftsmanship but in everyday life as well.

A good toy gives scope for a child's imagination. It should be pleasant both to look at and to feel. Corners should be rounded off, surfaces should be smoothed, colours should be bright. Toy bricks of uniform shape, colour and size leave little scope for a child's inventiveness, literally bringing him up against a brick wall. On the other hand, unusual shapes, semi-circular, triangular, irregular bits of wood resulting from off-cuts, fire a child's imagination and he can find a hundred uses for such pieces.

A good toy often provokes childish laughter (the Acrobat or the Ziggedy Man) or it is instructive in an interesting way (the Spinning Jenny and similar toys which work by balance).

Children love toys which allow free play to their imagination and which they can turn to all sorts of other uses than those intended by the designer. Much can be learnt from discreet observation of children with their playthings, and modifications and developments can be made as a result of their ideas. The approbation of a satisfied child is a wonderful incentive to further creation and nothing is more rewarding to a toymaker than to be told that a child has insisted on taking his toy up to bed with him!

Equipment

overcome this is the Mitre Block which can be bought quite cheaply and which is almost indispensable when a right-angled cut or a cut at 45° is required.

The mitre block consists of two rectangular pieces of wood glued together in an L shape, like the bottom and one side of a box. In the centre of the upright piece of wood is a saw-cut, or narrow slit, at 90°. To left and right of it are saw-cuts at 45°.

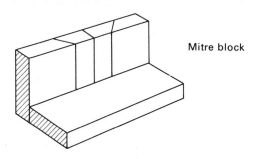

Mitre block

The first essential is either a work-bench or an old, steady table, with a top which projects sufficiently over the legs to enable clamps and vices to be fixed to it. It is advisable also to have a cutting board, which you can make for yourself, to protect the surface of your table. It looks like an elongated Z. The board could be 12 inches long by 6 inches wide in $\frac{1}{2}$-inch thick wood. At one end glue a 6-inch piece of wood $1\frac{1}{2}$ inches deep, and at the other end of the board and in the other direction glue a 6-inch piece of wood 3 inches deep. This enables one end of the block to be hooked over the edge of the table while the other edge is used as a stay for the wood you are cutting. It is also a help to make a saw cut in the end block at 90° as this angle is often needed.

A piece of wood is laid across the horizontal piece to prevent sawing into the block, and on top of it you place the piece of wood you wish to cut. Hold it firmly or clamp it down and then saw through the slit from the outside.

You can also buy a mitre box, which has an additional side to it. The ends are dead square as guides for cutting and the slits at 45° on opposite sides are lined up so that you can cut diagonally across from side to side. The block and the box can be held in a vice, or clamped or screwed to your table or bench.

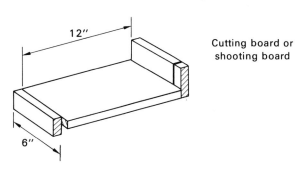

12"

6"

Cutting board or shooting board

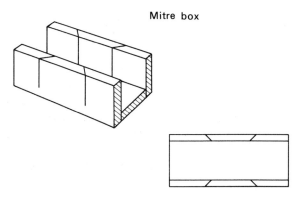

Mitre box

As it is always difficult to saw straight lines without a guide of some sort, another device to

Another very useful aid to sawing is a jig which consists of a flat piece of wood about 6 inches long, with a block of wood glued to it at either end at right angles. In the centre of these end-pieces you have previously cut out a V-shaped piece of wood, so that you can rest round wood, such as dowels of different sizes, or broom handles, for ease in cutting. (It is very difficult to control round wood without such a device.) You may very likely invent other aids for yourself as the days go by!

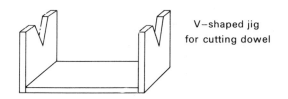

V−shaped jig
for cutting dowel

A piece of peg-board (hard board with holes drilled in it) mounted on a frame with golf-tees for pegs, and fixed to the wall near your table so that you can hang up pliers, hammers and other tools, is a great help to tidiness and to finding the necessary tool quickly. Screws and nails can be kept in plastic or glass jars with screw-on tops and kept on a shelf where they are easily seen; or a hole can be drilled in the lid, and the lid screwed into the under side of a shelf or a beam above your head, if the ceiling is low, and the jar of nails then screwed into the lid. This keeps your bench uncluttered and the contents of the jars clearly visible.

And now for a few tools. You will need a tenon saw,

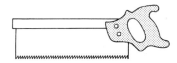

a hack-saw,

a fret-saw (with a largish bow if jig-saw cutting is undertaken) and a fret-cutting table, which is a small piece of wood or metal about 6 inches by 4 inches with a V-shaped opening, to be clamped or screwed to the table, so that the wood which you are shaping can rest on it and your fret-saw has clear movement.

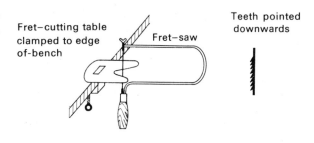

Fret−cutting table
clamped to edge
of-bench

Fret−saw

Teeth pointed
downwards

Also necessary are one or two small G-cramps and a vice for holding work, a hand-drill with a series of bits, and a counter-sink bit, which is needed for hollowing out the top of screw-holes so that screw heads do not protrude and scratch small hands.

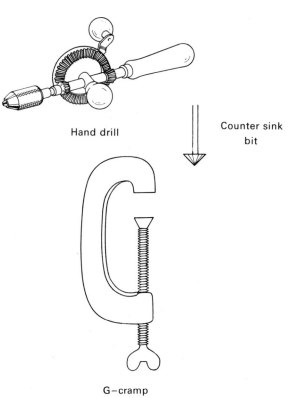

Hand drill

Counter sink
bit

G−cramp

9

You will need a good-sized flat wood file and several smaller ones, round files of various sizes for enlarging holes and rounding off, sandpaper of various grades from coarse to fine, and good glue. There are so many good glues available that I will be content with recommending my own favourite. It is Evo-Stik Wood Working Adhesive which is easy to handle. This is a white, creamy resin substance, easily wiped off while still wet, and sets firm as a rock in ten to fifteen minutes. It is equally good for sticking material to wood (e.g. ribbons in the Waterfall, p. 18). It is a good idea to squeeze out the amount wanted into a tin lid and apply it with a small flat stick shaped to a point: or, for sticking ribbon to wood, fold a piece of firm paper the width of your ribbon, dip one end in the glue and wipe it on to the ribbon. Bostik Carpentry Adhesive is similar in appearance and effect, and both these glues are easily washed off one's hands.

A see-through plastic ruler is essential; and a very helpful tool indeed is a metal ruler with a groove down the centre of one side. This groove carries a metal arm with a spirit level on it, a short rule at right angles to the long ruler, and also a short rule at 45° to the long ruler. This is called a Combination Try (90°) and Mitre (45°) Square.

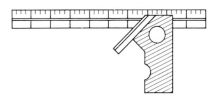

You will need a Try-square, pliers, a small and medium size screw-driver, a small hammer and a sharp penknife. It is a good habit to keep a sharply-pointed pencil and an indiarubber in your pocket and always replace them there because they will otherwise find a hundred hiding places on your bench. You will also need a pencil-sharpener, a compass, and Sellotape about $\frac{1}{4}$ to $\frac{1}{2}$ inch wide for strapping pieces of wood together, so that you can get drill holes and two parts of a toy exactly matching. With

this equipment any of the toys in this book can be made.

Of course, toy-making is made much easier and more efficient by the use of even one machine tool such as a drill and—to go with it and highly desirable—a stand for sanding (sandpapering). Later perhaps a drill stand for precision drilling as well. These are minor luxuries which would become necessities if toys are to be made in any quantity, but are not essential in the ordinary way. Certainly it saves endless time and work if sandpapering can be done by machine. The noise may be a little alarming at first, but you soon get used to it, and you learn to hold on tight to your piece of work so that it does not fly out of your hand!

A treadle fret-saw, or a power fret-saw, makes the work much quicker and easier, in the same way as an electric sewing machine rattles through stitching at far greater speed than a machine turned by hand. But expensive equipment is certainly not necessary to start with and much can be done with a few basic hand-tools.

Surprisingly little wood is needed in most of these toys and all of them can be made out of ply-wood, which is strong and easy to obtain in varying thicknesses. I do not recommend Meranti plywood for toys, as this fractures very easily when drilling holes, and splinters round the edges, but Birch or Beech ply are both very satisfactory.

Timber Merchants often have boxes of scrap wood to which you can help yourself, and practise on, or make things with.

Your timber-merchant or Do-It-Yourself supplier can save you a lot of time and work if you ask him to cut out your big pieces for you to the exact size, such as the frame for the Ziggedy Man or the base for Spinning Jenny.

For the Walking Duck and Walking Platypus, Parana Pine $\frac{1}{2}$ inch thick is ideal, especially if you can get a piece with the lovely red grain in it, otherwise ply or ordinary pine would do.

Dowel rods have a hundred uses and are needed in most toys. They can be bought by the foot in varying diameters from $\frac{1}{8}$ inch to $1\frac{1}{4}$ inches and should be chosen carefully as they vary within their sizes, and you want to

10

have the exact size dowel to correspond with your drill hole.

Half-round dowel $\frac{3}{4}$ inch wide and $\frac{1}{2}$-inch wood is needed for the Acrobat ($\frac{1}{2}$-inch wood is wood which measures $\frac{1}{2}$ inch by $\frac{1}{2}$ inch, i.e. it is square and is sold in lengths as you require it) and "Single Track" is needed for the ladder of Tumbling Tommy. All these things can be obtained from Do-It-Yourself shops and it is well to keep a small supply handy because you will always find a need for them.

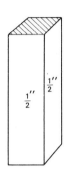

Painting, varnishing and waxing

Painting is a very enjoyable part of toy-making and a very important one. Children love bright colours, but the colours should harmonise and a few simple rules should help to achieve this. Unfortunately there are many people who say "I cannot paint!", and leave it at that. I did myself until I was shown, and began to practise, certain experiments in colour, which were so fascinating that my inhibitions gradually dissolved and working with colour became a joy instead of a pain! This is no uncommon experience, and for those who have had similar difficulties, I would suggest trying out the following ideas, based on Goethe's Theory of Colour, which have been developed in a book called *Goethe's Theory of Colour Applied by Maria Schindler* (New Knowledge Books, 1964).

There are three primary colours: these are yellow, blue and red, and you can find their complementary colours by means of a very interesting little experiment.

Paint a disk of red colour on a piece of white paper and gaze at it intently. After a short time its complementary colour—green—will appear circling round it. The green is luminous and fugitive and may not appear at once to everyone, it sometimes requires a little practice and perseverance. The moment when you first perceive it is an exciting one, and you realise you

have seen what is known as a physiological colour, one created by your eye in response to your concentration on a given colour.

You can also gaze at your red circle for several seconds and then move your gaze to a piece of white paper and you will see a whole green circle appear upon it. Your eye has created not only the complementary colour but also the form of a circle!

Similarly if you gaze at a blue disk, an orange complementary colour will appear, and if you gaze at a yellow disk, a violet complementary colour will appear. What is very remarkable, if you think about it, is the fact that you are experiencing a trinity in colour; for each single primary colour produces a complementary colour which is composed of two colours. Red produces green which is a combination of blue and yellow. Blue produces orange which is a combination of red and yellow. Yellow produces violet which is a combination of blue and red.

The opposite effect will also arise: if you gaze at a violet (blue and red) circle, your eye will create a yellow light around it. If you gaze at a green (blue and yellow) circle, red will appear, and if you gaze at an orange (red and yellow) circle, blue will appear. A little such practice with the colours will soon reveal to you which colours complement each other and awaken your interest in the fascinating phenomena of colour and its infinite variety.

Of course, there is much variation in the shade of each colour and you will soon discover, if you did not already know, that red, for instance, varies from a blue red, crimson, to scarlet which is an orange red, and you will then take scarlet as the correct red to combine with lemon yellow to give the best orange colour. Crimson red combined with ultramarine blue gives purple. Prussian blue combined with lemon yellow gives the best green. White will lighten and brighten any other colour.

It is also very good for removing one's inhibitions, and very interesting, to experiment with painting with liquid water colour on wet paper. Immerse a piece of drawing paper in a bowl of water and spread it on a drawing board or a piece of hardboard and smooth off the superfluous water with a small sponge, leaving the paper without wrinkles. Squeeze some lemon yellow water-colour into a little dish and drop some water on to it with a big brush. Mix it well and start painting it in a wide band across the centre of the page, trying to get an even distribution of the colour. When you have covered a third or more of your paper with this central band of yellow, wash your brush thoroughly and, starting from the top of the page, apply some liquid scarlet, and paint it evenly across your page until it meets with the yellow and gives you orange. Take care to keep your red, orange, and yellow distinct but smoothly blended where they meet (and to do this well requires care and practice).

Now in the same way start painting prussian blue (not too strong a mix!) up from the bottom of your page to meet the yellow, where it will, of course, turn to green, and you now have five of the seven colours of the rainbow in their proper sequence. All sorts of exercises can be developed along these lines, gradually bringing in form by using the blue for rocks, mountains or water and so on. Experiment with other colours too, prussian blue and ultra-marine as a seascape and skyscape together, crimson and ultramarine, blue and orange and so on, gradually letting the colours "speak" to each other. You will be astonished how much there is to these apparently simple exercises and how much you will learn from them and be helped in every way.

Very fascinating effects can be obtained by dipping a paint-brush full of lemon yellow water-colour into a jam jar of water and watching the clouds of colour that swirl about; then add some liquid prussian—not too much, it is very powerful—and, magically! green appears, weaving and intermingling in the water. If in this way you experiment with other colours too, you will learn a great deal about their pro-perties and will begin to take a new delight in them.

The question of what type of paint to use on toys is a little difficult because, at the time of writing (1972), manufacturers of artists' mate-rials are not required to state whether or not their paints contain poisonous substances. The only way to be certain is to write to the manu-facturers for information.

Generally speaking, I prefer Water Colours to Poster Colours or Oil paint, because the two latter tend to produce a more opaque effect, concealing the grain of the wood. For my own toy-making I consulted Messrs. Winsor & Newton about their Cotman Water Colours and they informed me that these are now all completely non-toxic and conform to the re-quirements of the Department of Education and Science Memorandum 2/65. I find these colours very satisfactory and the range is wide.

The Educational Supply Association recom-mend Finart Powder and Finart Liquicolour, which would be non-toxic, but I have not tried them out.

Food dyes, such as cochineal and other colours, are bound to be safe, but they, like all stains, are difficult to control and would only be suitable where a uniform surface, as for a table or stand, is required.

Although it is possible to mix most shades of colour from a basic set of two yellows (lemon and chrome); two blues (ultramarine and prussian); two reds (crimson and scarlet); and white and black; and it is also most valuable and enjoyable to experiment with colours in this way, I would nevertheless recommend for convenience and for saving time, that, in addi-tion to these 8 basic colours, you include in your collection an emerald green, a lilac, and a burnt umber (brown) and maybe a good orange as well. That makes a dozen tubes of colour in all, from which you can create dozens and dozens of colourful toys in all possible shades to rejoice your hearts and the hearts of your children and friends.

The best way to use them is to squeeze a small amount of paint on to an old plate and have a jar or two of clean water handy, and a paint rag too. Take a little water on your brush and mix it into the edge of the paint until you get the consistency you want. Always wash your brushes thoroughly when changing from one colour to another, and use clean water (keep changing it) so that the colours never become messy.

Painting on wood is a little different from

painting on paper and it is well to practise on scrap wood first. Make your wood really smooth by first damping it, allowing it to dry, and then sandpapering it. Do not apply the colour too wet, use fine paint-brushes except when there is a large surface to be covered, and you will soon find your way. When the paint is absolutely dry the work should be given at least one coat of clear varnish with a soft brush. Polyurethane varnishes are considered safe and, to my mind, a matt or egg-shell finish is preferable to a high gloss. When the varnish is absolutely dry, it may need another coat. Afterwards, when it is thoroughly dry, a little wax rubbed in and polished off with a soft rag will give the work a fine finish and make it smooth and pleasant to handle.

The best wax is one you can make for yourself from pure beeswax and distilled turpentine. But **be very careful indeed** for it can all too easily catch fire. Melt the beeswax in a flat tin, on an asbestos mat, over a very low heat. *Remove from heat* when melted and slowly add enough turpentine to make a soft wax when cool (about five tablespoonsful of turpentine to one ounce of wax) and stir it together. This makes a soft polish which is easy to apply and should be used sparingly. It should be kept covered to prevent it from getting hard. If your wax is too hard when it is set, you must melt it again and add more turpentine when it is melted, but being even more careful than the first time, because the wax and turpentine are still more highly inflammable. It is always a good idea to have an old plate handy to smother the flames if it catches fire!

A final word about painting. It is very important to give pleasing expressions to the faces you paint, and not to put in too much detail. The ends of mouths should curve upwards, a dot is sufficient for an eye, and with a slightly curved eyebrow, that is enough for a face.

Hair styles are amusing and easy to paint and help to give a softening and pleasing effect. It is fascinating to decide, with your paint-brush poised, whether to create a blonde, a brunette, a red-head, or a raven-black beauty!

Riveting

Rivet set

Riveting is required for the Doll and the four succeeding toys (Scissors, Nessie, the Owl and Angus). It is not a difficult process and with a little practice you can soon become expert.

The rivets should be made of aluminium which is a soft metal and easily bent over. For the toys in this book, small round-headed $\frac{1}{8}$-inch aluminium rivets have been used and $\frac{1}{8}$-inch steel washers. The length of rivet will be indicated with each toy.

A very satisfactory method is to use a quite inexpensive tool called a Rivet Set. It is simply a flat piece of metal, 4 inches long and $\frac{1}{2}$ inch thick with a cup-like depression (which can be of different sizes) on top: and which you fit into a vice.

Attach the pieces of wood you have to join by putting a rivet through them, leaving $\frac{1}{8}$ inch sticking out (if there is more, cut it off with pliers). Then lay the round head of the rivet into the cup-like depression of your Rivet Set (which is fixed in the vice), put a $\frac{1}{8}$-inch steel washer round the piece of rivet showing upwards, and gently tap around the end of the rivet with a hammer so that you spread this soft end over the washer sufficiently to prevent the washer from coming off.

A still neater job is obtained if you buy a second Rivet Set and lay the cup-like depression on it over the projecting end of the rivet.

Then give one or two firm taps to the Rivet Set and you will find it has rounded off the rivet very smoothly. Where movement is required in a toy, do not make your riveting too tight.

If a very loose joint is required, as in the Owl and "Angus", use a slightly longer rivet and insert a piece of thin metal between the parts you are joining. To do this you would require to drill out a $\frac{1}{8}$-inch hole in the metal and cut a short channel to meet it. (This you can easily do with your fret-saw.) Slip the metal in before you rivet and withdraw it when you have rounded off the end of rivet on to its washer.

Metal $\frac{1}{16}''$ thick

Drilling

Drilling must be done slowly and at right angles to the work, withdrawing the drill from time to time to blow out the accumulated sawdust which can deflect the drill. If a sloping hole is required (as in the three-legged stool given here), the *wood* must be arranged at the angle required and the drill kept upright.

If a large hole is required, start by drilling out a small central hole first, then gradually step up the size of the drill until you arrive at the size of hole you want. The wood should be turned over from time to time to prevent splintering on the under side, and to check that the hole is coming through dead centre where you want it to be.

Useful reminders

Always give pleasing expressions to faces and do not put in too much detail. Leave room for a child's imagination.

Countersink screw-holes.

Wrap sandpaper round a small block of wood for ease in sanding. Always sand *with* the grain of the wood.

Never do things in a hurry!

Be Exact!

When cutting two similar parts of a toy, such as two arms or two legs, trace your pattern on to wood and then strap your wood with Sellotape to another piece of wood similar in size, shape and thickness, and cut the two out together.

Always drill holes when required *before* cutting out.

Before painting on wood dampen it, let it dry and then sandpaper it.

After painting or varnishing small parts of toys with drill holes in them, thread them on to fine knitting needles and suspend them over a bowl to dry off.

Use plastic string in bright colours for joints wherever possible; it gives extra colour and security to your toy and saves using screws. A little touch of glue on the knot will prevent it from coming undone. And do you remember how to tie a reef knot which does not slip, instead of a granny knot which does?

Make toys pleasing to the touch as well as to the sight.

The magic
waterfall

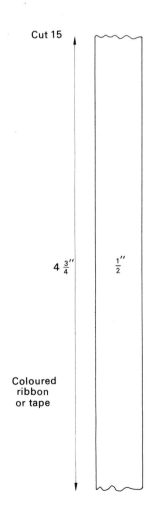

Cut 15

$4\frac{3}{4}''$

$\frac{1}{2}''$

Coloured
ribbon
or tape

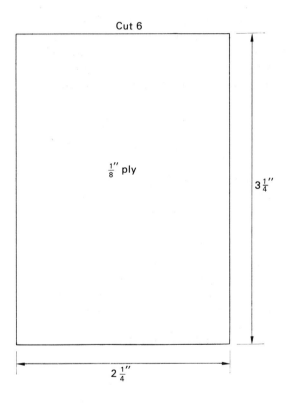

Cut 6

$\frac{1}{8}''$ ply

$3\frac{1}{4}''$

$2\frac{1}{4}''$

This is a very old and fascinating toy of Eastern origin and is the simplest possible toy to make. It only requires 6, or more, rectangular pieces of wood of identical size. They can be cut from plywood $\frac{1}{8}$ inch thick into pieces measuring $3\frac{1}{4}$ by $2\frac{1}{4}$ inches. (A Do-It-Yourself shop would supply strips of ply $2\frac{1}{4}$ inches wide from which you can cut off pieces $3\frac{1}{4}$ inches long.) For 6 pieces of this size, 15 pieces of ribbon or coloured tape $4\frac{3}{4}$ inches long will be required and to make a neat job it is advisable (but not of course essential) to cut the tape with a pair of pinking shears to prevent it from fraying. Five of the pieces of wood have three tapes glued to each, one central at one end, and two either side of centre at the other end. The last piece of wood does not carry tapes of its own.

Begin by attaching about $\frac{1}{2}$ inch of tape to the end of one piece of wood, A, in the centre, and $\frac{1}{2}$ inch of two tapes to the other end in such a way that there is clear passage for the central tape when the pieces of wood are joined up.

Now place A face downwards with the attached tapes underneath lying away from the piece of wood.

Bring them up from underneath and lay them along the wood.

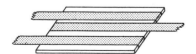

Put tapes on a second piece of wood, B, and place it exactly above A leaving its attached tapes spread out (underside downwards).

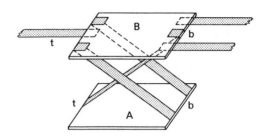

Now attach the single tape, which has come from the top end (t) of the *lower side of A*, to the bottom end (b) of the second piece of wood, B, on the *upper side*, and similarly attach the two tapes from the bottom end (b) of the *lower side of A* to the top end (t) of B *on the upper side*.

The tapes must be attached so that each piece of wood can lie exactly above the other, neither too tight nor too slack. (In the drawing the space between A and B is exaggerated for the sake of clarity.

Continue in the same way, putting tapes on C, laying it above B and joining B's tapes to C and so on until all six pieces of wood are joined together.

If the pieces of wood are coloured—and this makes the toy even more interesting and magic —say red on one side and blue on the other, then tapes will be attached to three pieces of wood of one colour and to two of the other. If red is face down to start with and blue is the side up, then the next piece of wood must be placed blue side down and red side up, and so on, *colour to colour*. This will ensure, surprisingly enough, that the toy will end up all blue on one side and all red on the other.

Obviously if you intend to make coloured waterfalls, the wood should be painted before being cut into pieces. Also, for speed, the five pieces of wood should have their three tapes attached before assemblage and remember, on three of one colour and two of the other.

To manipulate When all the pieces of wood are joined together, arrange them in a pile with the pieces of wood on which only the $\frac{1}{2}$ inches of tape show, at the top and bottom of the pile.

Pick the toy up by the top piece of the pile held between the first finger and the thumb, letting the other pieces fall downwards. Press the top piece gently downwards, forwards and then backwards, or backwards and then forwards, so that the tapes change over and each piece of wood seems to fall from the top to the bottom in turn. It is an illusion of course but a very convincing one!

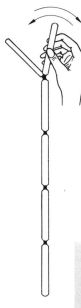

The climber

½″ wood
(½″ × ½″)

4″

Wood
½″ thick

Drill holes $\frac{1}{8}$″

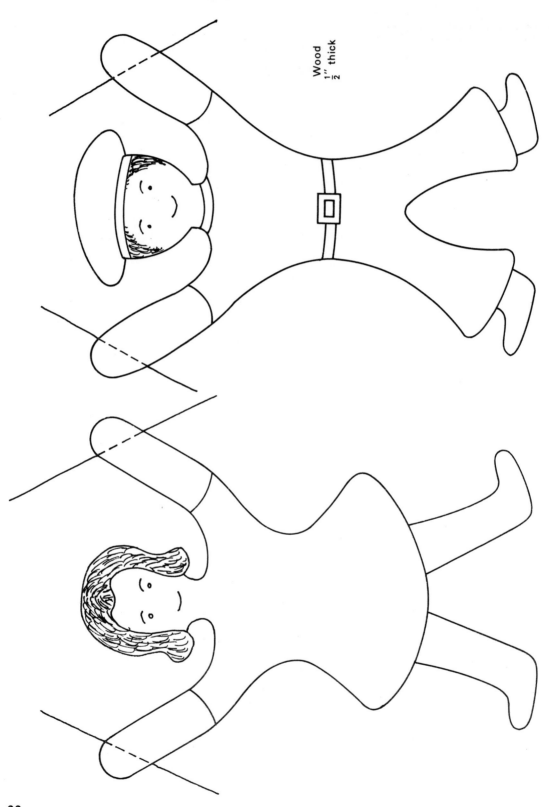

Wood
$\frac{1}{2}$" thick

Drill holes $\frac{1}{8}$"

Drill holes $\frac{1}{8}$"

22

This is a very clever toy much beloved by small children and it is simple to make. It can take many forms so long as the essential feature is there, which is a hole drilled at an angle through the end of out-stretched arms and through which strings pass from below to be fixed to either end of a bar of wood, which is suspended from a hook above, and must have free play to move up and down. By pulling on first one string and then the other, you make the climber mount rapidly to the top, to come down with a rush the moment the strings are slackened.

Cut out the figure in outline in $\frac{1}{2}$-inch thick wood as shown on the diagram, and drill $\frac{1}{8}$ inch holes in his hands at the angle shown in the drawing.

Cut off 4 inches of $\frac{1}{2}$-inch wood ($\frac{1}{2}$-inch wood is square, $\frac{1}{2}$ inch wide and $\frac{1}{2}$ inch thick) and drill three $\frac{1}{8}$ inch holes in it: one centrally, and one $\frac{1}{2}$ inch away from either end.

Thread about 3 to 4 feet lengths of blind cord, or string, through the bottom of each hand and through the end holes of the bar, from below, make a firm knot on top to hold it, and tie a bead to the other end of each of the strings.

Thread a short length of string through the central hole in the bar, fix it with a knot underneath and make a loop on top so that it can hang on a hook. Now test your climber and if he works well and climbs satisfactorily, take him out of the strings and paint him and varnish both him and the bar.

This is a very effective toy and simple to make, so long as the holes are drilled accurately, and the climber can perform a zig-zag movement up the strings. Three drawings are shown, the simplest is of prototype human shape, and the others are of a sailor and of a girl: other shapes can be worked out to suit the maker's imagination.

Thin blind cord, or plastic string, is suitable for threading through the holes, and the size of your drill hole will depend on the thickness of your cord. It should pass through easily but should not be too loose a fit.

23

The acrobat

The Acrobat requires a body, two arms, and two legs, cut from ⅛-inch plywood, a coloured wooden bead to keep his hands apart, and a frame to operate in, consisting of two pieces of half-round dowel kept apart by a small bar of ½-inch wood. Also required is some coloured plastic string to attach the limbs to the body, and the acrobat to the frame.

When cutting two arms and two legs which must match, it is advisable to draw out the shapes required on to one piece of wood and bind it to another of the same size with Sellotape so that you cut out two identical pieces at the same time. After the wood is strapped together, drill the holes where marked *before* cutting out the shapes. After cutting, strip off the Sellotape, make the surfaces very smooth with sandpaper, and paint and varnish them before putting them together. A simple way of drying them is to run a fine knitting needle through the holes and suspend the parts across a basin. When the parts are quite dry, put a double knot on a piece of coloured plastic string and thread first one leg on to the body and then the other, and make as close a knot as possible on the other side, and then attach the arms in the same way. NB. The joint should not be so tight that the legs and arms do not move freely, or the toy will not work well.

Meanwhile you will have made a frame by cutting two 9½ inch lengths of half-round flat dowel for the posts. Bind them together with Sellotape (flat sides together) and drill a small hole ½ inch from the top and another ½ inch below the first in the centre of the dowel; then a third hole, also dead centre, 2¼ inches from the bottom. Remove the Sellotape and smooth the pieces of dowel well, rounding off the corners top and bottom, and join them to a central bar 2⅜ inches long in which you have drilled a small hole centrally at either end. Apply glue to one end of the bar and then screw on one side with a ⅝-inch fine screw (no. 2) from the outside, and then do the same at the other side.

A better finish is obtained if, before putting in the screw, you widen the screw hole on the outside of the frame with a counter-sink bit so that the head of the screw does not obtrude and

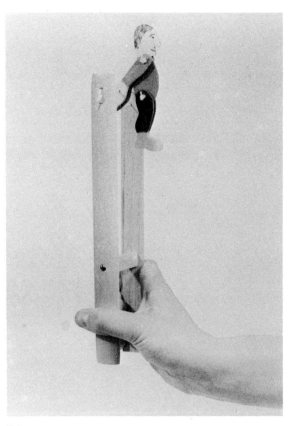

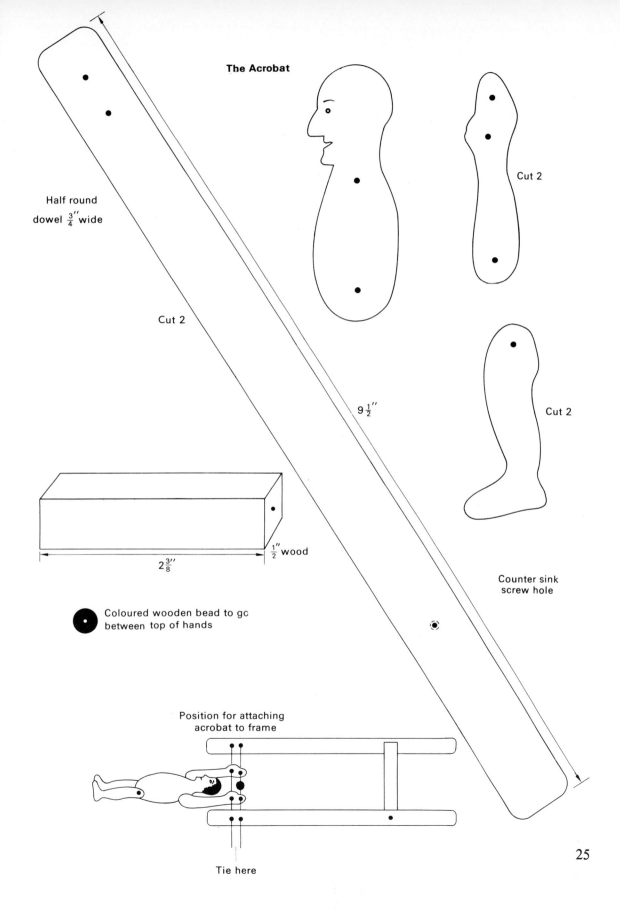

The Acrobat

Half round
dowel $\frac{3}{4}''$ wide

Cut 2

Cut 2

$9\frac{1}{2}''$

Cut 2

$\frac{1}{2}''$ wood

$2\frac{3}{8}''$

Counter sink
screw hole

Coloured wooden bead to go
between top of hands

Position for attaching
acrobat to frame

Tie here

25

scratch the hands of the manipulator.

Now attach the acrobat to his frame in the following way. Lay him face down or face up, it does not matter which, *away* from the frame, this is essential, with his hands inside the top of the frame.

Pass a thread from the outside through the lower of the two holes at the top of the frame, through the upper hole in the acrobat's hand, through the bead, then through the upper hole of the other hand and then through the lower hole on the opposite side of the frame. Bring the string back now through the remaining holes and tie it firmly together with the end of string left where you began. *Before fixing tightly, experiment to get the exact tension*; the distance between the posts should be about $\frac{1}{4}$ inch more at the top than the distance made by the fixed bar. When you hold the frame upright, the acrobat should now be hanging from strings crossed in two places. By gentle pressure and release at the *bottom* of the posts, he will perform somersaults and all sorts of fascinating acrobatics, by reason of the twisting and untwisting of the strings, which is known as the Torque principle. A touch of glue on the finished knots will prevent them from coming undone.

The gymnast

Begin by making a platform out of $\frac{3}{4}$ inch wood, about 2 by 3 inches, which you can shape to your fancy but into which you drill two holes (NB. It is easier to drill holes in a larger length of wood, so drill the holes before you cut out the individual platforms). The hole for the fixed post should be $\frac{1}{4}$ inch from the edge and $\frac{3}{8}$ inch in diameter, and the centre of the hole for the stick should be 1 inch away from the centre of the first hole, and should be $\frac{1}{2}$ inch in diameter.

Having drilled these holes, cut out the platform and smooth it well, rounding off the corners. Now cut two lengths of $\frac{3}{8}$-inch dowel, one $3\frac{1}{2}$ inches for the fixed post, which is the one nearer the edge of the platform, and one $9\frac{1}{4}$ inches for the movable stick. Drill a small hole in one end of each piece of dowel, to attach the hands and feet of the gymnast, and round off the tops. Glue the post solidly into the smaller, outer hole, with the drill holes at the sides.

Now make a little man, your gymnast, in the same way as for the acrobat only out of thicker ply, $\frac{1}{4}$ inch, and drill only one hole in his hands, near the top. Drill one hole in his feet a little nearer to his toes than just above the instep (see diagram). Paint and varnish him and string him together, rather more tightly than for the acrobat.

Attach your gymnast by the hands to the fixed post, and by the feet to the stick, which must first be inserted in the hole. Hold the platform in one hand and push the stick up with the other. You can thus make your gymnast stand on his feet or on his head or hands, dance, stamp, sit down and do other amusing feats. The length of the stick attached to the feet is calculated so that it cannot come out.

Incidentally, it may be interesting to record that the word "gymnast" is derived from a Greek word meaning naked. When I first made this toy I did not paint it and thought "gymnast" was a good name for his appearance and performance. Many people thought the toy was more interesting coloured, and I agreed, but have not changed the name, though for strict accuracy I suppose it should be called "the coloured gymnast"!

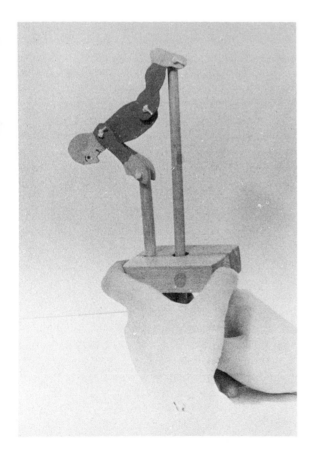

This toy is a development of the well-known Monkey on a Stick and is a great joy to small children.

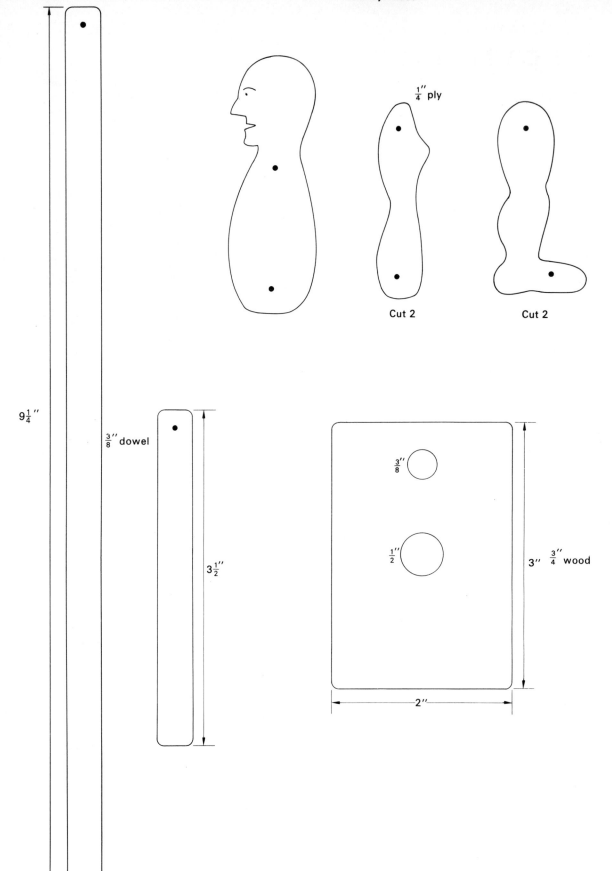

$\frac{1}{4}''$ ply

Cut 2

Cut 2

$9\frac{1}{4}''$

$\frac{3}{8}''$ dowel

$3\frac{1}{2}''$

$\frac{3}{8}''$

$\frac{1}{2}''$

$3''$ $\frac{3}{4}''$ wood

$2''$

The athlete

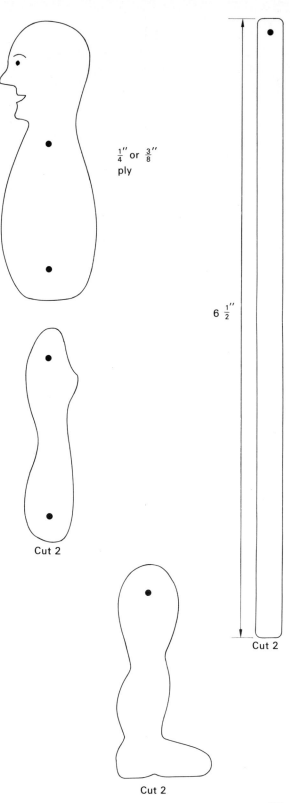

$\frac{1}{4}''$ or $\frac{3}{8}''$
ply

$6\frac{1}{2}''$

Cut 2

Cut 2

Cut 2

The Athlete is another variant of the Monkey on a Stick, the difference being that the Athlete's sticks are not fixed together. Although he is similar to the last toy, the Gymnast, he can do several different things; the potentialities of each are different.

Cut out the same size figure as for the Gymnast and paint and varnish him as before. Now cut two $6\frac{1}{2}$ inch lengths of $\frac{1}{4}$-inch dowel, round off the ends, and drill a small hole, $\frac{1}{4}$ inch from the end, in one end of each. Varnish the sticks and attach the athlete with coloured nylon string, by the hands to one stick, and by the feet to the other.

You will, I think quite enjoy playing with him yourself and finding out what he can do.

29

Tangram

The Tangram is a very old and fascinating puzzle which originated in China hundreds of years ago. It consists of a square dissected into seven pieces: one small square, five isosceles (two sides equal) right-angled triangles, two large and two small of identical sizes, and one of medium size; and one parallelogram.

From this one square cut up in this way, two smaller, identical squares can be made, as well as an infinite number of shapes representing men, women, birds, fish, animals, trees, boats and so forth. Some well-known ones are shown here, but their number is endless and you can probably discover many others for yourselves.

The easiest way to make the Tangram is to cut it from two squares. A 4 inch square is a good size and $\frac{3}{16}$-inch Birch is very suitable material.

Trace the drawings given on to your wood and cut out the pieces very carefully indeed so that your lines and angles are absolutely accurate. Keep the pieces together in a tin or box or plastic bag. The Tangram is a very interesting and instructive companion for young and old, especially during wet weekends, holidays, camps and so on.

Tangram arranged in 2 squares

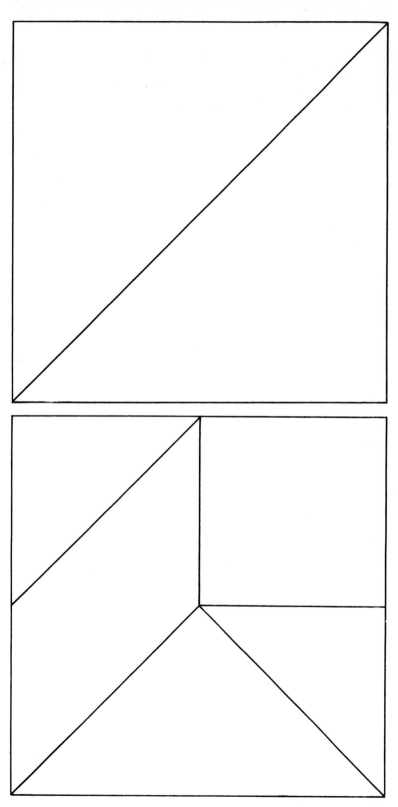

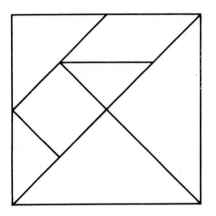

Various shapes made from a Tangram

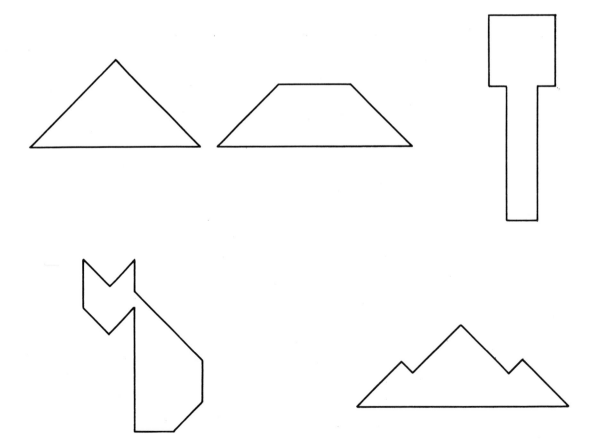

Table and stools

The Table is made from wood or ply $\frac{3}{4}$ inch thick, and is $8\frac{1}{2}$ inches long and $4\frac{3}{4}$ inches wide. Round off the corners and drill $\frac{1}{2}$ inch holes for the legs exactly as marked, aligned to each other as shown in the diagram. (As a check, draw lines parallel to each side $\frac{3}{4}$ inch from the edge; where these lines intersect will be the centre of your drill holes.) Cut the 4 legs, 5 inches long, from $\frac{1}{2}$-inch dowel, smooth the ends and glue the legs into the holes you have drilled, and you will have a fine sturdy table, which you can now paint and/or varnish.

If your table top is not made from a wood with an attractive grain which you want to keep, it is a good idea to cover it with a piece of one of the attractive Fablons or Con-Tacts now available. Cut the Fablon to size, spread glue over the table, take the paper backing off the Fablon and smooth the Fablon on to the table and press it down. This provides a ready-made tablecloth, easy to wipe clean after a dolls' tea-party.

Stools

It is easier to make a straight stool than a round one, and the measurements to go with the table are $\frac{7}{16}$-inch wood or ply, $3\frac{1}{2}$ inches long by $2\frac{1}{2}$ inches wide. (This measurement allows the stool to fit in between the legs of the table, top and bottom as well as at the sides.) Drill 4 $\frac{5}{16}$-inch holes where marked, cut the legs $2\frac{3}{8}$ inches long from $\frac{5}{16}$-inch dowel, smooth the ends and glue in the legs, and you have a very strong stool. A child, however, would probably use it as a table for smaller dolls, and it would be easy to make a still smaller stool of solid wood to go with it: the dimensions would be $1\frac{3}{4}$ by $1\frac{1}{8}$ by 1 inches. Round off the edges and varnish it.

A solid round stool could easily be made for the small table by sawing off $1\frac{1}{4}$-inch from 1-inch dowel and rounding it off, or by sawing off $1\frac{1}{4}$ inches from an old broom handle, which is usually made of pine 1 inch in diameter. Sand it well to bring up the grain and varnish it.

Larger round stools are very attractive but a little more difficult to achieve than straight ones. To go with the first table, a stool of $3\frac{1}{2}$ inches diameter in $\frac{7}{16}$-inch ply or wood is suitable. Drill 3 $\frac{3}{8}$-inch holes as marked and cut 3 lengths of $\frac{3}{8}$-inch dowel $2\frac{1}{2}$ inches long. The stool is much more attractive if the legs are slightly splayed outwards. To do this, put your stool top into the vice at a slight angle, about 20 degrees, sloping towards you, upwards, then holding your drill absolutely straight drill your hole, trying, for the sake of appearance, not to pierce the top of the stool; moving the stool top round at an angle for each hole you drill. Then glue in the legs and varnish, or colour and then varnish.

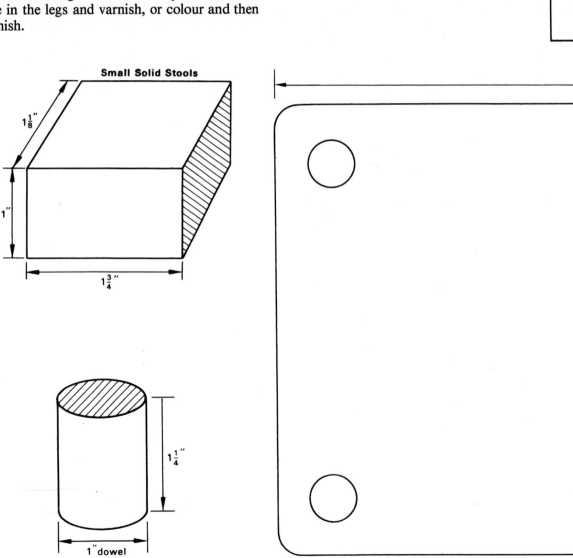

Small Solid Stools

$1\frac{1}{8}''$

$1''$

$1\frac{3}{4}''$

$1\frac{1}{4}''$

$1''$ dowel

Table

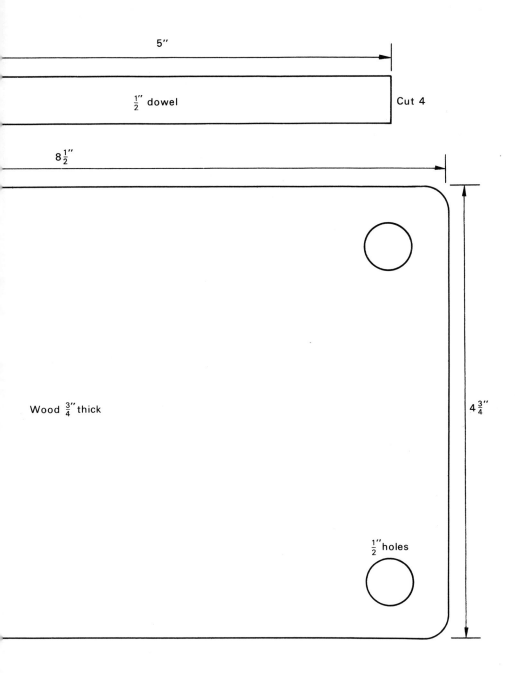

5″

½″ dowel   Cut 4

8½″

Wood ¾″ thick

4¾″

½″ holes

35

Cut 3

$\frac{3}{8}''$ dowel

$2\frac{1}{2}''$

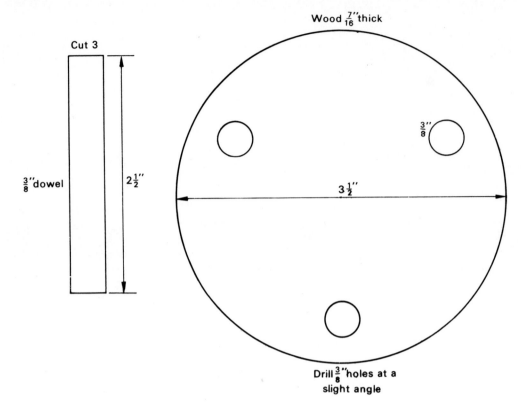

Wood $\frac{7}{16}''$ thick

$\frac{3}{8}''$

$3\frac{1}{2}''$

Drill $\frac{3}{8}''$ holes at a
slight angle

Wood $\frac{7}{16}''$ thick

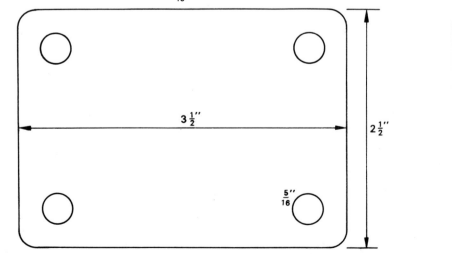

$3\frac{1}{2}''$

$\frac{5}{16}''$

$2\frac{1}{2}''$

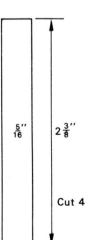

$\frac{5}{16}''$

$2\frac{3}{8}''$

Cut 4

Tumbling Tommy (p 66) climbs up his ladder, while

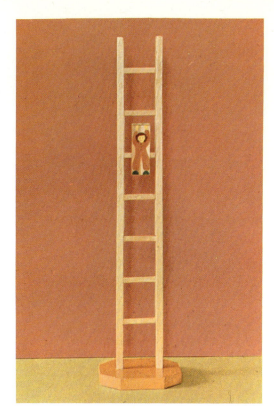

Ziggedy Man (p 64) falls down his board

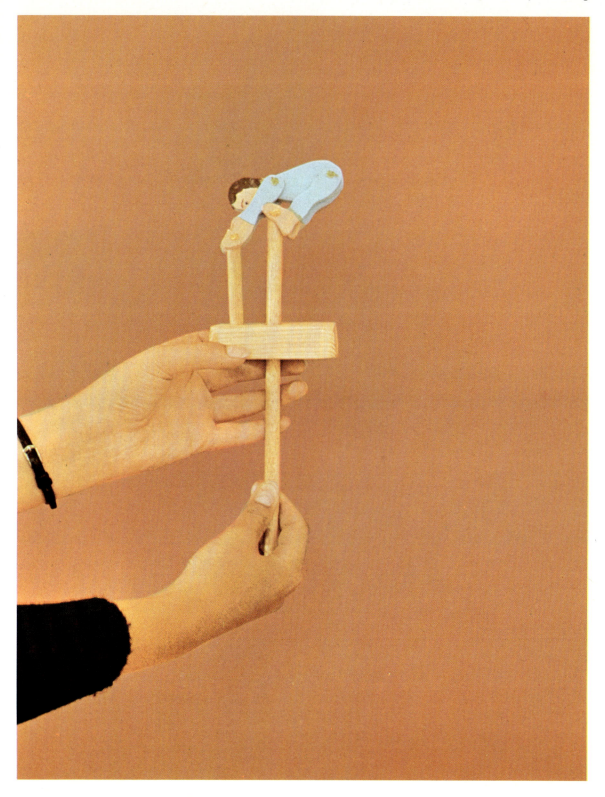

The acrobat (p 24)

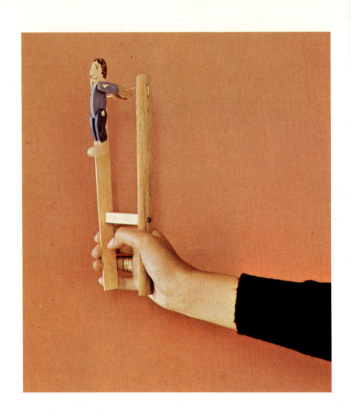

Nessie, the "scissors" toy (p 57)

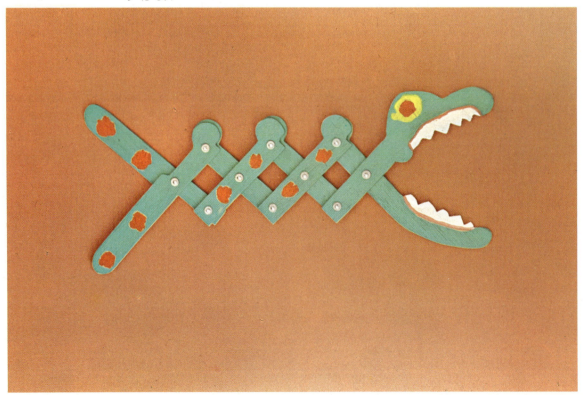

Spinning Jenny

and if Jenny is started gently up the slope, she will come back of her own accord. This is a very interesting toy to play with owing to its mysterious properties of balance.

The base of the frame for Spinning Jenny is the same size as the table in the preceding section, the only difference in the construction being the addition of parallel bars. Prepare the base and the legs as for the table and drill $\frac{1}{4}$-inch holes, $\frac{1}{4}$ inch from one end of each leg (or post) —dead centre! Round off the top of the post, smooth the work well and try fitting the ends of the parallel bars ($\frac{1}{4}$-inch dowel, 7 inches long) into the holes, rounding them off at the ends until they fit in snugly. Now glue in these ends to the posts, and the posts into the table, at the same time, being careful to get everything squared up correctly. The frame can now be varnished, or painted and varnished, as you choose, and a Fablon top glued on as well may-be, because it makes a good table as well as a frame and can become a dual purpose toy.

Now draw out the outline of Jenny on to $\frac{3}{16}$-inch plywood, taking care to mark in the drill-holes at the exact place. Drill the hole first and then cut out the shape with your fret-saw and sandpaper it well. Care must be taken to get the dowel rod through her with as close a fitting as possible, and, with the aid of glue, be sure that the rod is fixed absolutely tight and at right angles to her body. It is a good idea to mark the centre of the dowel before putting it through, then put a little glue in the hole to ease the dowel in, and before you get to the centre of the dowel, put a ring of glue around it for fixing; because the glue you began with in the hole will probably all have got worked away. Paint Jenny now, varnish her and let her spin to your heart's content. You may find it a help to painting to trace her outline on to paper and then cut away her hood and arms as indicated by the dotted lines. Lay this over Jenny and you will find, I think, that with this guide it is quite easy to get the shape of her sleeves and kerchief right. Leave her hands without paint, and paint her dress in one colour, say blue, and her sleeves and head-scarf in another, say crimson. Eyes, mouth and hair should be painted in too and when dry, varnished.

"Spinning Jenny" is my version of a well-known balance toy. In response to a gentle turn on the rod which goes through Jenny, and which she seems to be holding, she will move backwards or forwards along parallel bars. If one end of the frame is tilted upwards at a slight angle, by placing it on a book about half an inch thick,

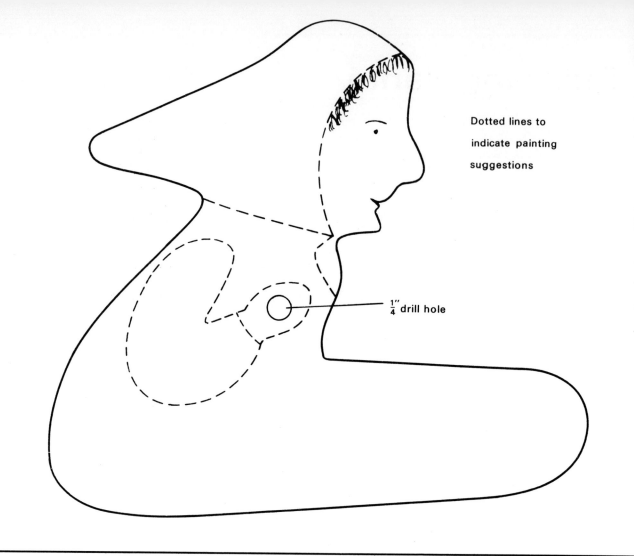

Dotted lines to indicate painting suggestions

$\frac{1''}{4}$ drill hole

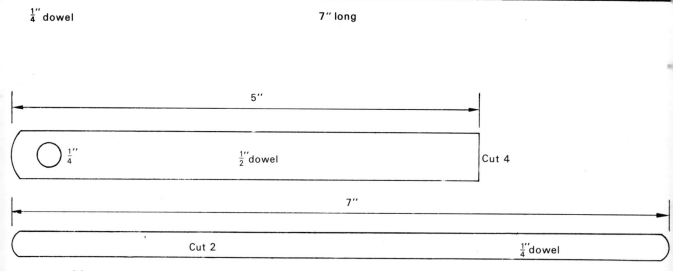

$\frac{1''}{4}$ dowel   7" long

5"

$\frac{1''}{4}$ $\frac{1''}{2}$ dowel   Cut 4

7"

Cut 2 $\frac{1''}{4}$ dowel

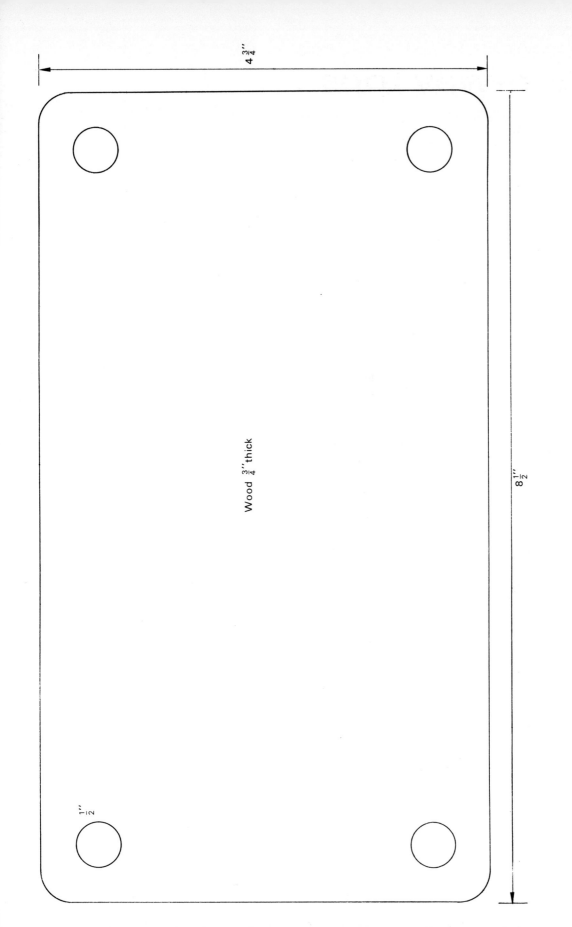

Wood $\frac{3}{4}$" thick

4 $\frac{3}{4}$"

8 $\frac{1}{2}$"

1 $\frac{1}{2}$"

39

Two-way tops

Very good tops, *which spin equally well on both sides,* can be made from ply $\frac{1}{8}$ inch or $\frac{3}{16}$ inch thick. The diameter to be 2 inches or $1\frac{3}{4}$ inches, the stalk is made from $\frac{1}{4}$ inch dowel, 2 inches long for the larger circle, $1\frac{3}{4}$ inches for the smaller one.

Draw out your circle on to the ply and drill a hole centrally $\frac{1}{4}$ inch wide. Then saw out the circle and smooth it well. Lightly shave off a little from each end of the dowel with two or three turns of a pencil-sharpener. (These tops do *not* need a sharp point to spin well.) Mark the centre of the dowel and put a little glue round it, and a little at one end to ease it into the hole, then fix the dowel firmly in, absolutely square to the circle of wood.

Test by spinning it that the top is in balance. Make any necessary adjustments and leave it till the glue is set. The top should spin silently; if it rattles, it is either out of balance or needing to be sandpapered.

Very interesting colour effects and colour blending can be obtained by painting these tops. For instance, a patch of crimson next to a patch of ultramarine blue will show as vivid purple when the top is spinning. Scarlet and yellow will make orange and so on. Dots of colour will merge into a ring.

If you have a hole-saw, you can, of course, use it to cut out your tops, or if you wanted to make a lot of them, it would be easy and inexpensive to have them turned.

If you find it difficult to saw a circle, a hexagon or a 6-point star as shown will do equally well. Incidentally it will look like a circle when it spins and this is interesting to note, and it is a little easier to cut out.

40

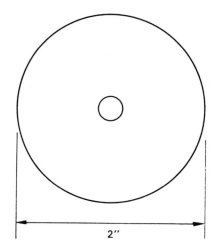

2"

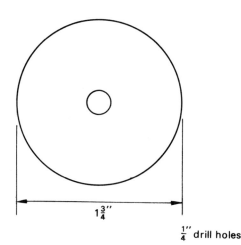

$1\frac{3}{4}''$

$\frac{1}{4}''$ drill holes

Two-way Tops

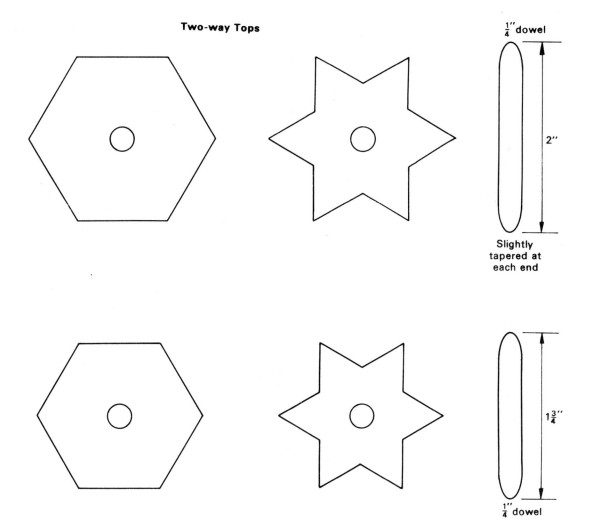

$\frac{1}{4}''$ dowel

2''

Slightly
tapered at
each end

$1\frac{3}{4}''$

$\frac{1}{4}''$ dowel

41

The walking duck

"Walking" Toys which move down a slope are enjoyed by the quite young child, even if he often carries the toy about and puts it to many other uses. These toys seem very simple to make, i.e. just drill the holes, cut out the shapes and fit them together and that is that. But I am bound to say it does not always work out in this way and the adjustment is very fine. You should succeed if you follow these patterns carefully enough. Accurate placing of drill holes, shaping of feet (drill and cut them together), the shape where the animal's body touches the ground, are the places where the most care is needed.

Do not glue in the legs until you are satisfied you have got good action, as the positioning is very critical. When the toy is complete the dowel should fit tightly into the legs, and just be able to revolve in the body, so the drill hole for the body is $\frac{1}{16}$ inch larger than the ones for the legs. Incidentally, if you make this body hole too large, the toy will not work any more than if the hole is too small!

When testing, after you have attached the legs (without glue as yet) to the body by putting the dowel pins through—and the legs should be square to, and as close to, the body as will permit of free movement, no washers are needed—hold the creature upright with the legs between your finger and thumb; the body should then be in balance, slightly tipping forward. Try walking him down a gentle slope. When the action is to your satisfaction, do any painting required and then varnish. When quite dry, glue the dowels into the feet, taking care not to get glue on to the body.

Walking Duck

Cut two

$1\frac{7}{8}$"

$\frac{1}{4}$" dowel

Cut two

$\frac{1}{4}$"
drill

Wood $\frac{1}{2}$" thick

$\frac{5}{16}$"

N.B. Drill hole on body $\frac{1}{16}$" larger than on leg

The walking platypus

The Platypus is very amusing when he walks well. He can walk backwards as well as forwards. The points to watch when making him are the same as for the Duck.

Both toys look delightful if made from Parana pine, which often has beautiful streaks of red in it. If you use wood with interesting grain like this, then the only painting necessary would be for beak and eyes in the Duck, and eyes and snout for the Platypus.

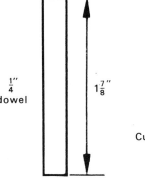

$\frac{1}{4}''$
dowel

$1\frac{7}{8}''$

Cut 2

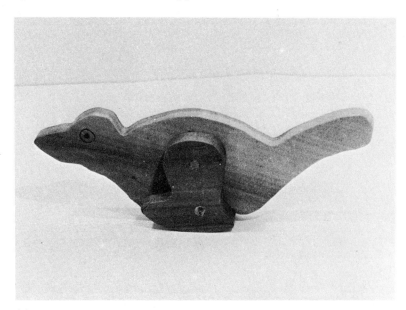

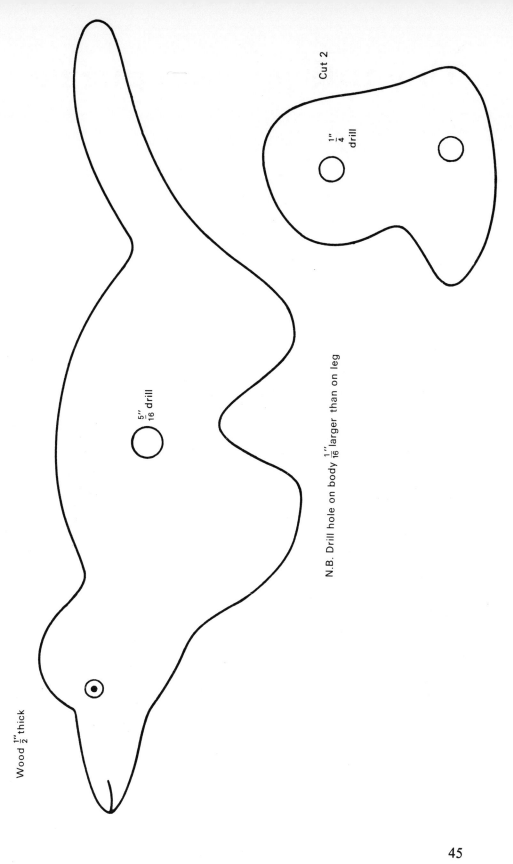

Walking Platypus

Wood $\frac{1}{2}$" thick

$\frac{5}{16}$" drill

Cut 2

$\frac{1}{4}$" drill

N.B. Drill hole on body $\frac{1}{16}$" larger than on leg

45

Tiny tots jig-saw puzzle

This four-piece jigsaw puzzle in thick wood ($\frac{3}{4}$ inch) was designed by a friend of mine. Small children love it, because in addition to the fun of putting it together, they can play with each piece separately, stand it by itself, or build it up with the other pieces in all sorts of ways.

If you can obtain a piece of iroko teak with which to make it, you will be very pleased with the result, as it has a beautiful golden colour, interesting grain, and takes paint and varnish well. Of course, any good wood will do, but it must be $\frac{3}{4}$ inch thick. Cut out the pieces, then paint the toadstool scarlet or crimson on top, with splashes of white. Give the gnome a white beard and white hair, a bright cap, and paint in sleeves a different colour to his suit, leaving his hands unpainted, resting on his tummy.

When the puzzle is complete, it can be made to stand on one or other of the cut-off corners, but that piece by itself will not balance on its corner, and it is of much interest to try and see how and where to put some other bit to provide a counterbalance.

NB. The illustration to this puzzle is on paper just a little bit too narrow and should be copied on to wood measuring $7\frac{1}{4}$ by $7\frac{1}{4}$ inches or even $7\frac{1}{2}$ by $7\frac{1}{2}$ inches. Place the drawing centrally on to your wood, leaving an even space all round. Project the horizontal line to the sides and cut

your way in from it. The extra space is needed to prevent the arches from fracturing when they are cut out, as they easily can if the wood is too narrow.

46

Tiny Tots Jigsaw Puzzle

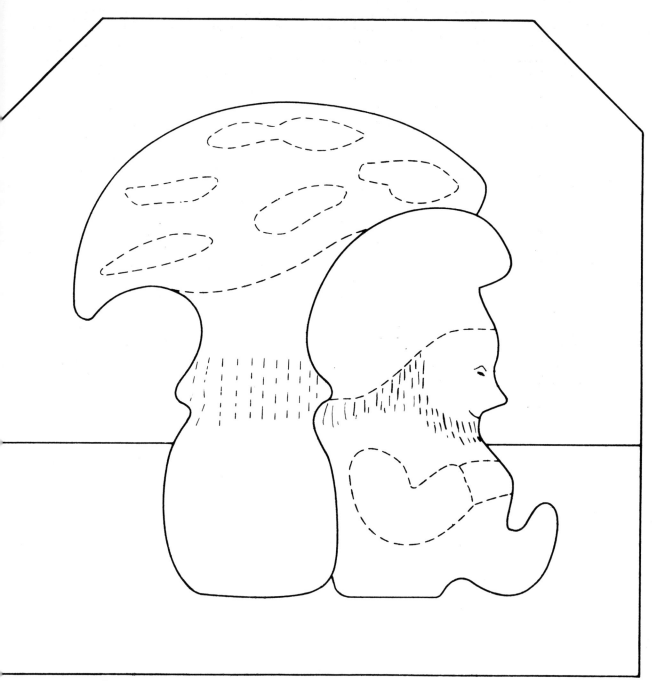

ᴐod $\frac{3}{4}$" thick, 7 $\frac{1}{4}$" by 7 $\frac{1}{4}$" (slightly larger than shown here) Dotted lines are indications for painting

47

Toys on wheels

A toy that can be pushed or pulled along is of great appeal to small children. It is not difficult to make a small trolley, say $4\frac{1}{2}$ inches long by 2 inches wide, or an engine with trucks linked behind. Wheels can be made by cutting 1-inch or $1\frac{1}{4}$-inch dowel into sections $\frac{1}{2}$ inch wide and drilling them centrally. A neat effect is obtained if you do not drill the hole all the way through but stop just beyond half way. Some cotton-reels, sawn in half, also make good wheels and so do large wooden beads. If larger wheels are required, you could have them turned to the size you want.

There are two ways of fixing wheels, but, to my mind, the first method described here is by far the best on a toy intended for small children. This is to glue one wheel (which you have drilled centrally to the size required) on to a dowel, pass the other end through the hole you have drilled in your trolley or truck and fix another wheel on to it. By this method, the wheels and the dowel to which they are attached, all revolve together.

If the trolley is more than one or two inches wide, it would be difficult to drill such a long hole, so runners or bearers of $\frac{1}{2}$-inch wood can be glued along the length of it underneath, and holes drilled for the dowel to pass through. Wheels attached in this way run perfectly satisfactorily without washers and are entirely safe for children to play with.

The other way to make wheels move is to let them revolve round an axle, which could be dowel, or a screw or a nail, which is fixed to the trolley or to its runners. But the wheel must be kept on! If the axle is of wood, then a split pin or a wedge could be used to do this; or if it is a nail or screw, then the head must do it and you would require to counter-sink it on the wheel. Instead of counter-sinking, you could drill out the top of your hole $\frac{1}{8}$ inch deep with a slightly larger drill, because the head of your nail or screw *must* be below the surface of the wheel to prevent any possibility of scratching. As it seems to me preferable never to use nails or screws in toys for small children, unless there is no other way of achieving the effect you want (and this is seldom the case) I recommend the first way of fixing wheels, though I have given directions for both.

The engine

Wood for Undercarriage—$\frac{1}{2}''$ thick, $1''$ by $3\frac{3}{4}''$

Boiler—$\frac{7}{8}''$ dowel, $2\frac{1}{4}''$ long

Funnel—$\frac{7}{16}''$ dowel, $\frac{5}{8}''$ long

Cab—$1''$ by $1''$ by $\frac{7}{8}''$

4 Wheels—$\frac{1}{2}''$ thick, cut from $\frac{7}{8}''$ dowel

2 Axles—$1\frac{3}{4}''$ long, cut from $\frac{3}{16}''$ dowel.

Drill $\frac{1}{4}$-inch holes centrally through side of undercarriage $\frac{3}{4}$ inch from each end. Shape the cab as shown in the diagram and round off the top. Drill a $\frac{7}{16}$-inch hole in the top of the boiler, $\frac{1}{4}$ inch deep, $\frac{1}{2}$ inch from the end. Paint the funnel red and glue it into this hole. Glue the boiler centrally on to the undercarriage, $\frac{1}{2}$ inch from the front. Glue the cab on to the other end and on to the undercarriage at the same time. Glue one end of the axles into the wheels, pass the other ends through the undercarriage and glue on the remaining wheels. (NB. The axle measurements are calculated for the wheels to be drilled just beyond halfway: if the hole is taken all the way through, the axle rods must be cut a little longer.) Fix a hook at one end and an eye at the other. Varnish, or paint and varnish as you prefer.

This is a sporting little engine which can be pulled along or which will gallop down a slope at great speed.

Engine

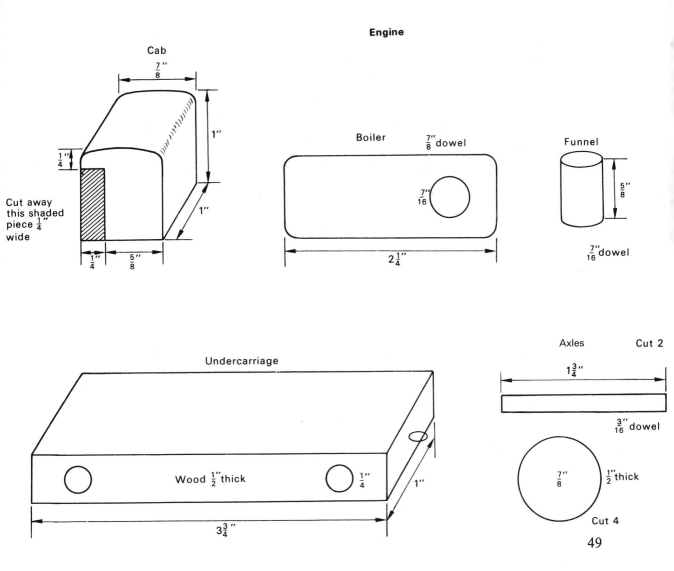

49

Tender

Wood for Undercarriage—$\frac{1}{2}''$ thick, $1\frac{1}{8}''$ by $2\frac{3}{8}''$
Wood for Sides and Back—$\frac{3}{4}''$ by $2\frac{3}{8}''$ by $1\frac{1}{8}''$
4 Wheels—$\frac{1}{2}''$ thick, cut from $\frac{7}{8}''$ dowel
2 Axles—$1\frac{3}{4}''$ long, cut from $\frac{3}{16}''$ dowel

Make the undercarriage and drill two $\frac{7}{32}$-inch holes through it $\frac{3}{8}$ inch from each end. Take the wood for the sides and back of the tender and saw out a piece centrally 2 inches long by $\frac{3}{4}$ inch wide (see diagram) curving it round at the back, and leaving the sides and back in one piece. Round off the open ends slightly, and glue this shaped piece on to the undercarriage; press under a weight for ten minutes. Fix on the wheels as in the engine, varnish, or paint and varnish, and put a hook and eye at either end of the tender.

Tender

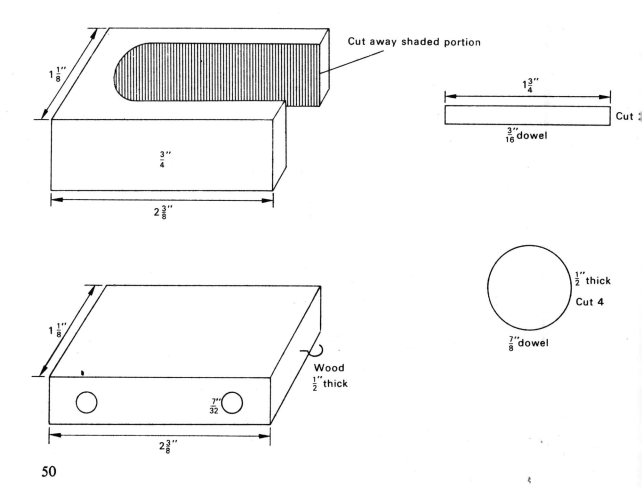

Cut away shaded portion

Simple little trolley

Wood—$\frac{1}{2}''$ thick, $2\frac{3}{4}''$ by $1\frac{5}{8}''$

4 Wheels—$\frac{1}{2}''$ thick, cut from $\frac{7}{8}''$ dowel, drilled right through centrally with $\frac{1}{8}''$ drill

4 1″ nails.

Prepare the wood and round off the corners. Drill holes with $\frac{3}{32}$-inch drill a short way only, $\frac{1}{2}$ inch from each end, and drill small holes back and front for hook and eye. Counter-sink the holes in the wheels so that the nail heads are received into them. Make sure that the wheels revolve freely on the nails, then tap them gently home, leaving sufficient space for the wheels to revolve freely. Finish with hook and eye fore and aft.

This toy is very quick and easy to make and the measurements could be altered to suit the toymaker. It does not matter which side is uppermost, which is intriguing to a small child.

Simple Little Trolley

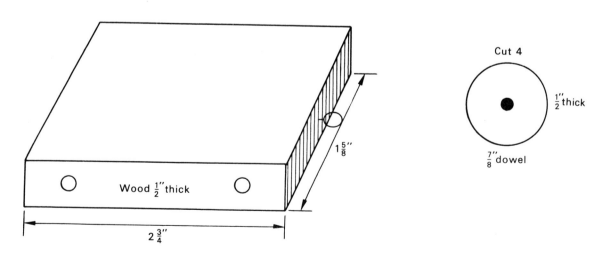

51

Wagon

This is a slightly larger, slightly more complicated toy than the last but perfectly simple to make.

Undercarriage—$\frac{3}{8}''$ wood, $4\frac{1}{4}''$ by $2''$
2 Bearers—$\frac{1}{2}''$ wood, $4\frac{1}{4}''$ long
4 Wheels—$\frac{1}{2}''$ thick, cut from $\frac{7}{8}''$ dowel, drilled right through with $\frac{11}{64}''$ drill
4 1″ screws—No. 4
Sides of Wagon—$\frac{1}{8}''$ wood, $4\frac{1}{4}''$ by $\frac{5}{8}''$
Back and Front—$\frac{1}{8}''$ wood, $2''$ by $1''$

Drill—not quite halfway through—two $\frac{11}{64}$ inch holes in the sides of the bearers $\frac{3}{4}$ inch from either end. Drill $\frac{11}{64}$-inch holes centrally right through the wheels.

Glue the bearers along the bottom of the undercarriage and—to strengthen the join—drill two $\frac{1}{8}$-inch holes $\frac{1}{2}$ inch each side of the centre, through the undercarriage and halfway through the bearers. Glue $\frac{5}{8}$ inch lengths of $\frac{1}{8}$-inch dowel into these holes, and leave all this to set for ten minutes pressed under a weight.

Meantime cut out the sides and two ends of the wagon, and when the first part of the work is set, glue the sides and back to the top and to each other. Counter-sink the outside holes of the wheels and screw them into the bearers, leaving sufficient space for them to turn freely. Screw in a hook and eye at either end.

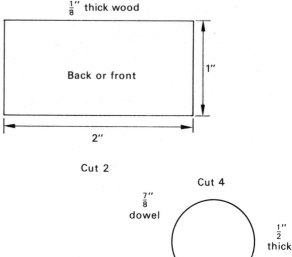

$\frac{1}{8}''$ thick wood

Back or front

$1''$

$2''$

Cut 2

Cut 4

$\frac{7}{8}''$ dowel

$\frac{1}{2}''$ thick

$\frac{11}{64}$

Drill and countersink

$\frac{1}{8}''$ thick wood

Side

Cut 2

$\frac{5}{8}''$

$4\frac{1}{4}''$

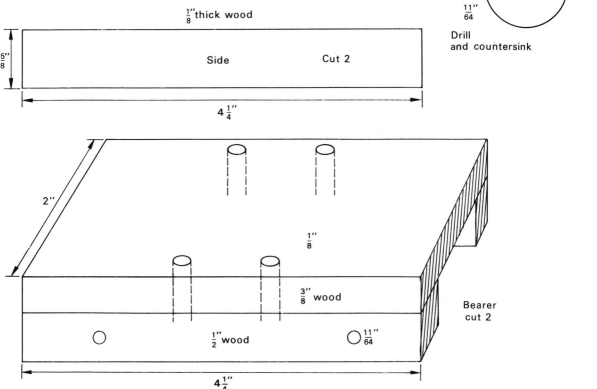

$2''$

$\frac{1}{8}$

$\frac{3}{8}''$ wood

$\frac{1}{2}''$ wood

$\frac{11}{64}$

Bearer cut 2

$4\frac{1}{4}''$

52

The doll

The Doll is made from $\frac{3}{16}$-inch ply. Draw out the pattern on to your wood and lay the piece of wood over another piece identical in size, and bind the two firmly together, either with Sellotape, or by drilling out holes top and bottom and at the sides, and dropping in a rivet or a piece of cane or fine dowel the exact thickness, to hold the pieces of wood together while you saw. Drill the holes as marked for joining the arms and legs to the body, and then cut out carefully the five pieces. Smooth them well,

paint them and varnish them. When dry, fasten them together by means of rivets $\frac{1}{8}$ inch diameter and $\frac{3}{4}$ inch long. The joining should be loose enough to allow the limbs to move freely but firm enough for the doll to stand upright without collapsing.

This doll is of the right size to sit on the small stools at the small table (large stool) already described, and it can be made to adopt all sorts of interesting postures.

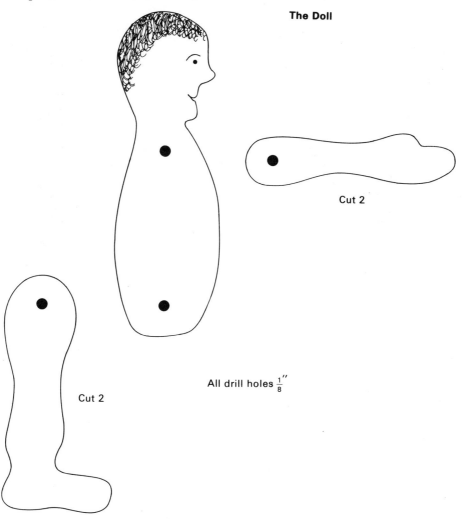

The Doll

Cut 2

Cut 2

All drill holes $\frac{1}{8}''$

53

Scissor toy

This is my variation of the well-known Scissor Toy. It works from either end. It is not really difficult to make though it requires exactitude; its symmetry and movement are most satisfying. The success of the toy depends on the pieces of wood being of the exact size indicated, and the positioning of the drill holes identical; so the pieces of wood should be drilled together at the same time and not separately. Chickens and hens are often used as decoration on this toy but I have found that golf tees are effective, they lend colour and interest to the folding and unfolding of the scissors, and they are easy to fix. I suggest golf tees because they are easily obtained from Sports Shops, but coloured wooden or plastic pegs would be suitable too.

The easiest way to make this toy is to obtain 1 inch wide ramin $\frac{1}{8}$ inch thick and you will require 4 feet, perhaps a little more in case of slight mistakes! Ramin is a hard wood, easily obtainable, cut into varying widths and of varying thicknesses. Of course, the toy can equally well be made from $\frac{1}{8}$-inch ply, but if so, you must be sure to cut your pieces in the length of the grain, and you may have a little more difficulty in making them an exact match.

Begin by cutting out your pieces of wood the exact sizes required, smoothing them well and rounding off the ends of the longer pieces as shown in the diagram. Mark off the holes exactly as shown, on one of the shorter pieces, and bind it firmly on top of the other five pieces with Sellotape. Then drill the $\frac{1}{8}$ inch outside holes and the centre hole only. Undo these six pieces and lay one of them exactly above one end of the four long pieces. Bind them together and drill through two holes only, the one $\frac{3}{8}$ inch

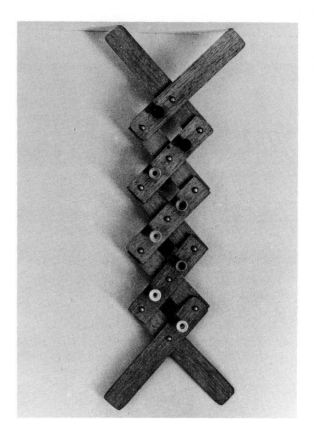

from the end, and the centre hole of the short piece.

If you would like to put in golf tees as ornament, you should now take three of the shorter pieces, bind them together with the one marked out on top. Keep them firmly together by slipping in a rivet or a piece of cane into the existing holes and drill a $\frac{3}{16}$-inch hole through the two places marked ($\frac{13}{16}$ inch each side of the central hole). Now lay one of these pieces over *two* of the longer pieces, keep them all together as above, and drill a $\frac{3}{16}$-inch hole through them,

54

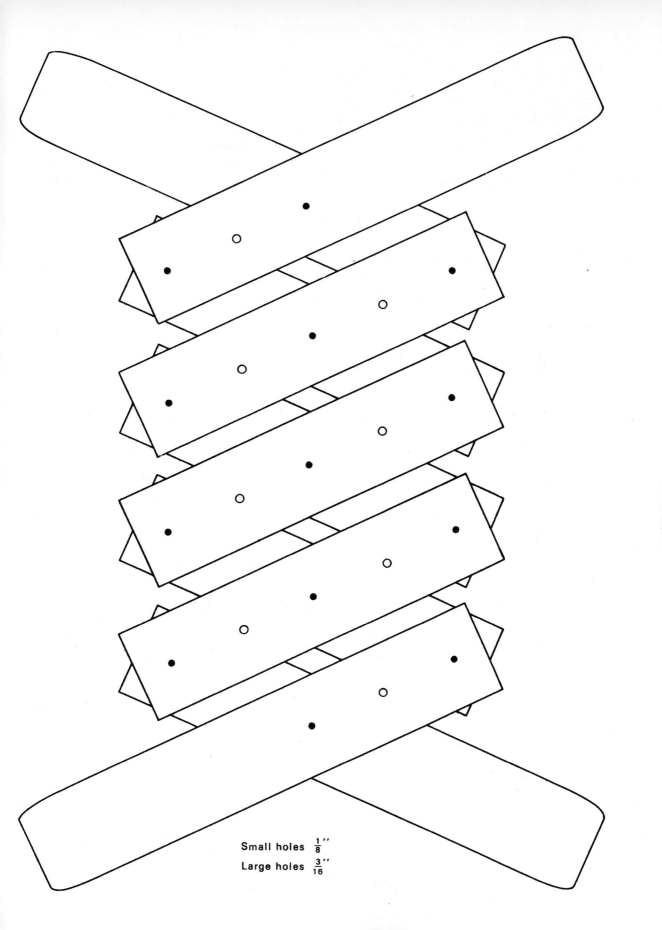

Small holes $\frac{1}{8}''$

Large holes $\frac{3}{16}''$

between the two holes already drilled. Fit golf tees into the eight holes you have made, cut them off on the wrong side and smooth off the ends, but do not glue them in yet. Take them out again once you have prepared them and lay them aside until you join the scissors together by means of $\frac{1}{8}$-inch rivets $\frac{1}{2}$ inch long, tapping the headless end over on to a steel washer (see p. 15).

It is a little tricky at first to remember just which piece to join to which, but the diagram should keep you right. Remember there are five pieces on top running parallel to each other and five pieces underneath running parallel to each other in the opposite direction. The top pieces will carry the golf tees (if you have decided to put them in).

You will, I feel sure, be delighted with the way the scissors work when you have done the riveting—which should not be too tight—and you will appreciate the need for precision. Now glue in the golf tees, keeping the same order of colour on each side, say white, yellow, blue, red. It is fascinating to watch their changing positions as the scissors move.

Nessie

"Nessie", the nickname given to the Loch Ness Monster, was evolved by a friend and myself when we were trying to think out a good Souvenir for Scotland in a recent Competition. She is made on the principle of the Scissor toy, with the addition of a jaw with some teeth, and three humps! Children enjoy this toy very much, and it is great fun to make and to paint. There is a little less riveting than in the previous one because there are only eight pieces instead of ten.

Owing to the shape of Nessie's jaws and humps, it would not be practical to cut her from ramin and she should be cut from $\frac{1}{8}$-inch ply, making sure that the grain is running lengthwise. You will find that six of the pieces carry a hump at one end and only two do not—one tail piece and the upper jaw. Care must be taken to arrange the humps correctly when assembling the toy, and also to position the holes exactly when drilling. They should be $\frac{3}{8}$ inch from the ends and $1\frac{5}{8}$ inch apart.

Cut out the pieces carefully, drill holes in the four shorter pieces which carry the humps, by binding them together first and then drilling them at the same time. Use one of them for marking off the holes in the other pieces. Smooth them well, then paint and varnish them before riveting them together, again not too tightly to check the movement of her snapping jaws!

Paint Nessie green and dab some red spots on her. Paint her teeth white and her gums pink. Give her a large bright red eye surrounded by bright yellow; make her look gay rather than fearsome!

Nessie

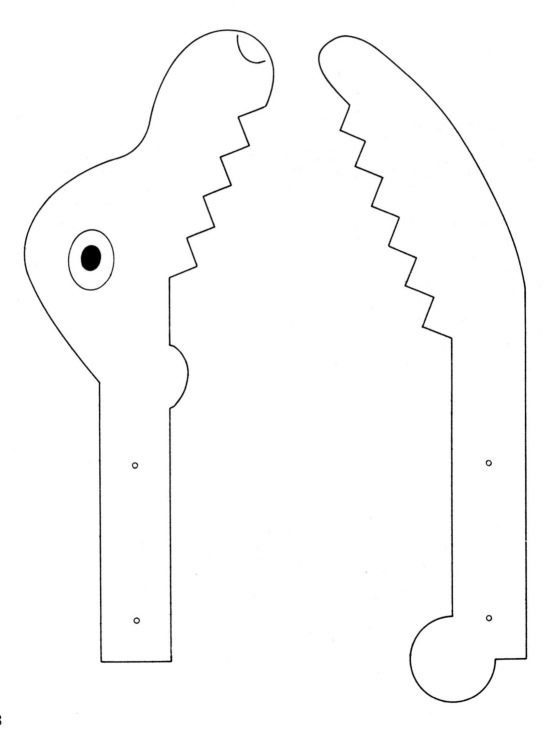

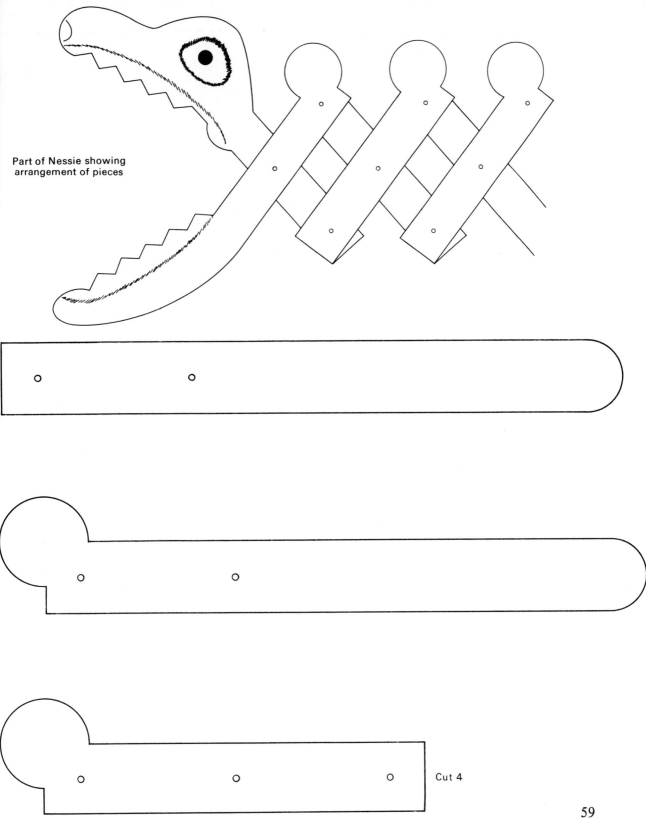

Part of Nessie showing
arrangement of pieces

Cut 4

59

The owl

Cut 2 ears

This is a fairly simple toy to make and it gives much pleasure to both children and grown-ups: good painting is very important to give the best effect. Cut out the five pieces shown and drill the holes as marked. Smooth the wood well and paint and varnish the owl on to it. Knot a loop of fine string or linen thread into each of the four small holes, leaving about $\frac{1}{2}$-inch loop protruding. Rivet the wings and ears loosely on to the Owl, thread strings through the loops you have already made. Tie the strings into position, leaving about three inches hanging down. Join the strings through a bead at the bottom; tug gently and watch your Owl perform. Thread a loop of string through the hole in his head and hang him up on the wall.

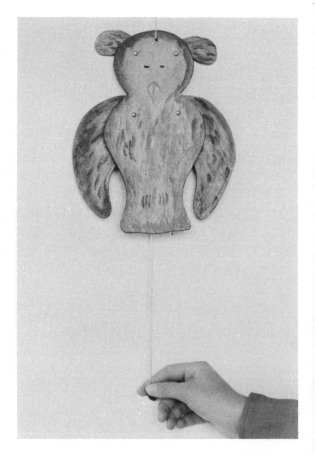

60

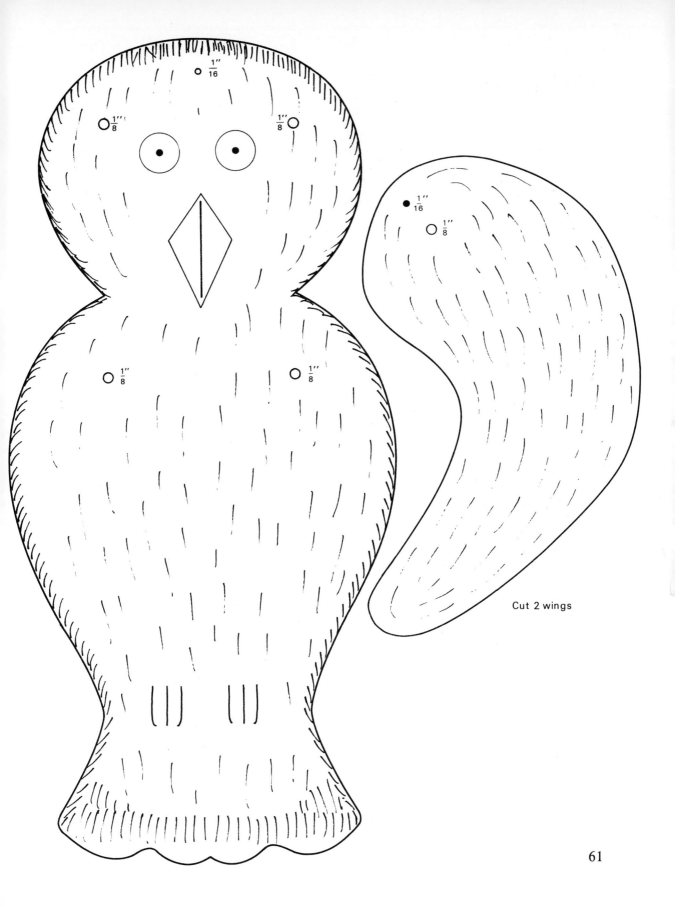

Cut 2 wings

61

Angus

Angus was devised at the same time as Nessie for the Souvenir for Scotland Competition. He was dressed in tartan Fablon (which can now be obtained in red and green) back and front, and he performs some fine capers, Highland Fling steps with some Russian dancing thrown in, but he is much quicker to make if he is just painted.

Draw out the seven pieces as shown on a piece of $\frac{1}{8}$-inch plywood. Lay the plywood over a similar sized piece, holding the two together with Sellotape or panel pins. Drill the holes as marked and cut out the pieces. Smooth them well and paint them and varnish them. Make small loops with linen thread or very fine string at the four places marked, and join the parts loosely together by riveting, putting the body over the arm and thigh pieces, and the thigh pieces over the lower legs. These joints must be very loose so that Angus can cut his capers; so you will have to insert a thin strip of metal between the parts as you rivet, to make enough space for the arms and legs to move freely. Finish by attaching separate strings to the loops of arms and of legs, leaving a few inches dangling down and ending with a bead of different colour on each. Make a loop to go through the top of his head and put Angus through his paces!

If you want to make a tartan version of this toy, it is advisable to glue the tartan Fablon to your wood back and front first of all, trying to match the pattern on each side, and leaving a clear space of wood top and bottom for the head, hands and feet. (It is endless labour to try and glue the Fablon on to the separate pieces once they are cut out.) If you make a tartan Angus, make your drill holes at least one size larger, because the Fablon checks the movement. Paint round the sides of the various pieces to match the colour of the tartan, and give him a bright bonnet and black shoes. Finish off with strings as before and your braw Hieland man will dance to your bidding!

Angus

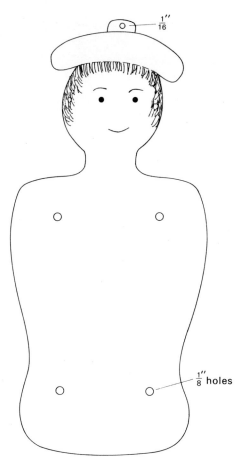

$\frac{1''}{16}$

$\frac{1''}{8}$ holes

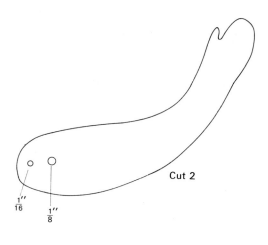

Cut 2

$\frac{1''}{16}$

$\frac{1''}{8}$

$\frac{1''}{8}$ plywood

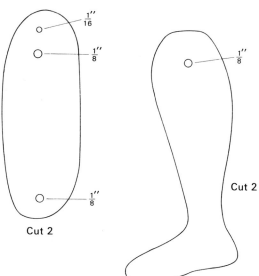

$\frac{1''}{16}$

$\frac{1''}{8}$

$\frac{1''}{8}$

Cut 2

$\frac{1''}{8}$

Cut 2

63

Ziggedy man

The Ziggedy Man has outstretched arms and uses them to move in zig-zag fashion, and with a pleasant clickety sound, down a board which has two parallel lines of projecting golf tees, or wooden pegs, set at an angle to each other. He requires a board of $\frac{1}{2}$ inch thick plywood 2 feet long, 4 inches wide, and 18 golf tees. The man himself can be cut from either $\frac{1}{8}$-inch or $\frac{3}{16}$-inch plywood.

This is a delightful toy in action and is not difficult to make but it does demand absolute precision.

Cut the board—or have it cut at a Do-It-Yourself shop—to the required measurements, round off the corners and smooth it very well.

Draw lines parallel to the sides $\frac{3}{4}$ inch from each side to keep your drawing in check, then lay the chart exactly over the board and mark through with a compass point the bottom two holes, $\frac{3}{4}$ inch from the bottom. Then mark off the others: on the left-hand side, the second hole and all the others will be at $2\frac{3}{4}$ inches from each other. On the right-hand side the second hole up will be $1\frac{3}{8}$ inch above the bottom one, and the others will follow at $2\frac{3}{4}$ inch distance.

Continue marking the holes along your parallel lines $2\frac{3}{4}$ inches apart until there are 9 hole marks on each side. Make very sure that the mark for each hole falls along the parallel lines and that the distances are exact. Use a compass or dividers for certainty. Drill out the holes with a $\frac{3}{16}$-inch drill and glue in golf tees, leaving about $\frac{5}{8}$ inch sticking up. Snip off the remainder of the tee at the back of the board and smooth it all over. (Golf tees vary in size but the average one will go just far enough into a $\frac{3}{16}$-inch hole to leave about $\frac{5}{8}$ inch sticking up.) Drill a small hole centrally $\frac{1}{2}$ inch from the top of the board and insert string for hanging it up. Varnish the board. Now cut out of $\frac{1}{8}$-inch or $\frac{3}{16}$-inch ply a little man according to the diagram, smooth him well and test him on the board. Make any necessary adjustments, then paint him with bright colours and a cheerful expression and varnish him.

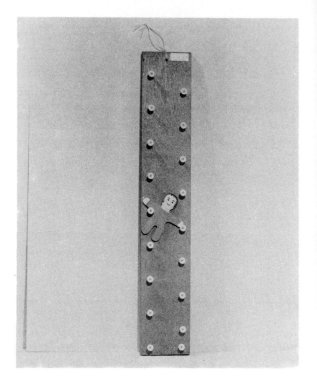

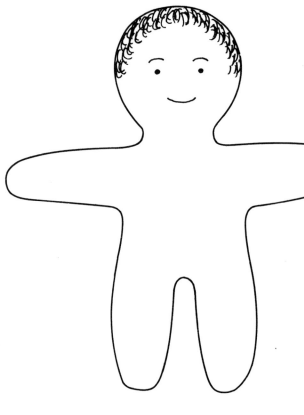

$\frac{3}{16}''$ plywood

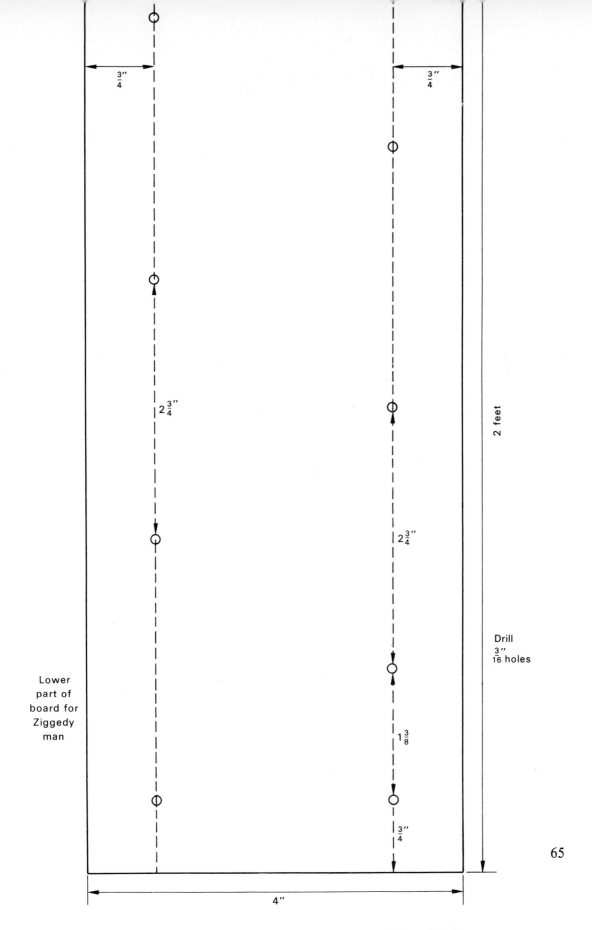

$\frac{3''}{4}$

$\frac{3''}{4}$

2 feet

$2\frac{3''}{4}$

$2\frac{3''}{4}$

Drill
$\frac{3''}{16}$ holes

Lower
part of
board for
Ziggedy
man

$1\frac{3}{8}$

$\frac{3''}{4}$

65

4''

Tumbling Tommy

This toy demands patience and great exactitude in its construction and for that reason I have kept it to the last, but it is most rewarding and satisfying to make. It is not suitable for very small children because the measurements should be so exact that Tommy can only start from the top or the bottom of the ladder, and the young child wants to push him in anywhere. It seems to me best for six years old and upward.

You will require:

7 Rungs from $\frac{1}{8}''$ ply, $\frac{3}{8}''$ wide, $2\frac{3}{4}''$ long
12 Supports—$\frac{1}{8}''$ ply, $\frac{1}{4}''$ wide, $2\frac{1}{2}''$ long
2 Supports—$\frac{1}{8}''$ ply, $\frac{1}{4}''$ wide, $4\frac{1}{4}''$ long
Base—$\frac{3}{4}''$ thick wood or ply $5\frac{3}{4}''$ by $5\frac{3}{4}''$
2 Sides—24″ inch lengths of Single Track, or Single Channel, $\frac{1}{2}''$ wood

Begin by preparing the rungs and supports. You can make your rungs of ramin, a hard wood which you can obtain $\frac{1}{8}$ inch thick, in three sizes $\frac{1}{2}$ inch, 1 inch and 2 inches wide. You can either buy the $\frac{1}{2}$ inch width and cut an eighth off it to obtain the right width for the rungs, and divide some of the ramin down the middle to get the $\frac{1}{4}$ inch width you need for the supports; or you can buy the 1 inch width and cut it into three strips, two of $\frac{3}{8}$ inch width and one of $\frac{1}{4}$ inch. This is the more economical way, for then you can use it all, but it requires fine cutting.

The sides of the ladder are made from "single track or single channel $\frac{1}{2}$-inch wood" (this is $\frac{1}{2}$-inch wood which has a $\frac{1}{4}$ inch deep channel down its length) and you will require two 24 inch lengths, the tops of which you should round off.

The base is made from $\frac{3}{4}$ inch thick wood or ply and a good size is $5\frac{3}{4}$ by $5\frac{3}{4}$ inches. It looks best if it has the corners cut off as shown in the diagram. It can be coloured brightly and varnished.

The holes for the uprights should be $2\frac{1}{4}$ inches apart and placed centrally in the base as shown. To cut out the half inch squares required, drill a hole large enough to insert the fret-saw blade, one end of which will have to be disconnected from your saw, inserted in the hole and then reconnected. Cut out the squares, file smooth and test that the posts fit in satisfactorily, the channels to the inside, of course. Glue them into position making sure that they are standing squarely. Slip a rung into the top of the ladder and then put a strong elastic band round the top to keep the posts parallel while you build up the ladder.

To do this, glue in the two long ($4\frac{1}{4}$ inch) supports from the bottom, slipping them into the channel from underneath through the base.

Now glue in a bottom rung to rest on top of them. Then glue in two supports ($2\frac{1}{2}$ inch) into the channels on top of the rung, on each side and continue in this way until the ladder is completed. Bind a string tightly round the top to keep the rungs in place until the glue is set.

As a result of putting in these supports, not only is a very strong ladder obtained, but the rungs will be absolutely true and equi-distant from each other; and this is difficult to obtain by other methods. Varnish the ladder and its painted base and it is now complete.

Now that the ladder is made, you must turn your attention to Tommy. He is made out of a piece of wood $1\frac{1}{4}$ inch wide, $\frac{7}{8}$ inch deep and $3\frac{7}{16}$ inches long.

Mark a line down the centre of the narrow $\frac{7}{8}$ inch side and mark off one inch from either end and this will give you the position of the bottom of the $\frac{7}{16}$-inch holes you will have to drill (the holes will be $\frac{9}{16}$ inch away from each other). NB. It is quite difficult to drill a $\frac{7}{16}$-inch

Tumbling Tommy

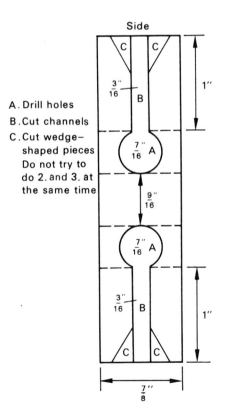

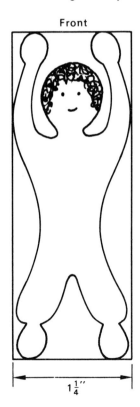

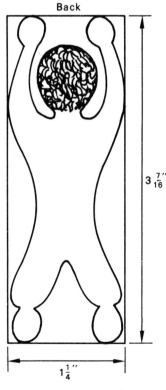

67

hole as deep as $1\frac{1}{4}$ inches and keep it dead straight, and this is what you are required to do! Drill a small hole first centrally, and then slowly and carefully, keeping your drill absolutely straight, enlarge your holes with intermediate size drills until you get to the $\frac{7}{16}$-inch drill. Check the hole from the other side from time to time to make sure it is central. It is a good idea to practise first on a piece of spare wood. When the holes are made, cut a central channel $\frac{3}{16}$ inch wide from either end to meet them. Then half-way down these channels make a sloping cut to the ends, leaving them $\frac{1}{8}$ inch thick. Smooth the surfaces with sandpaper and Tommy should now tumble satisfactorily from rung to rung. If so, paint the figure back and front and varnish it, and when dry, just sit back and play and enjoy your triumph!

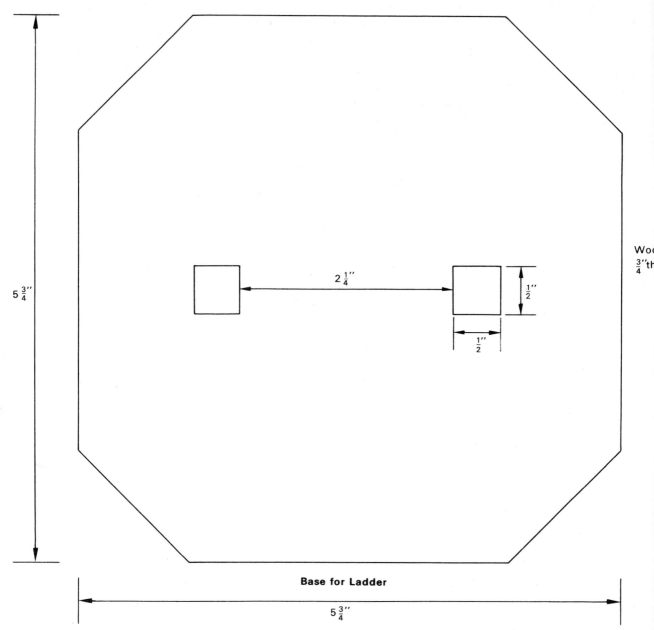

Base for Ladder

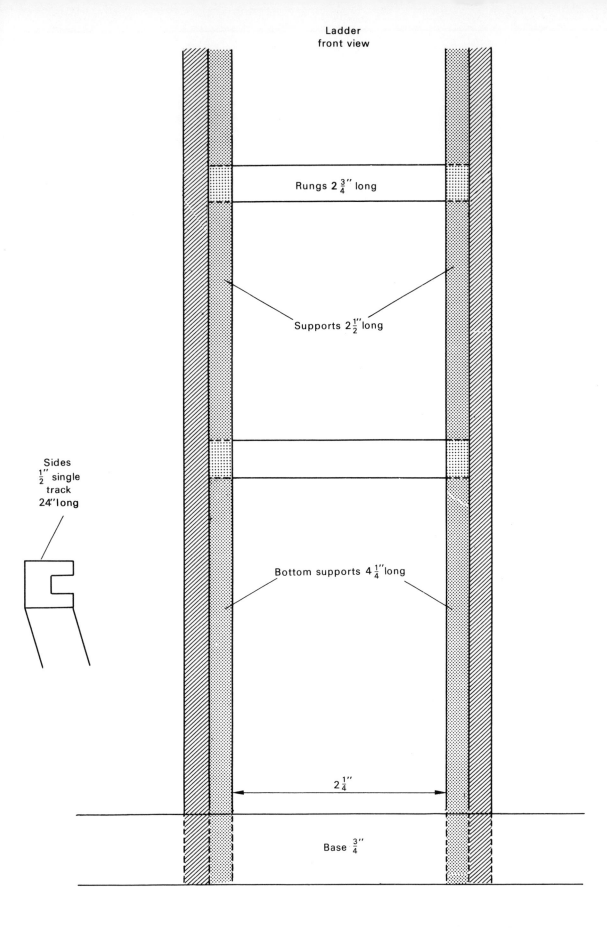

Ladder
front view

Rungs $2\frac{3}{4}''$ long

Supports $2\frac{1}{2}''$ long

Sides
$\frac{1}{2}''$ single
track
24″long

Bottom supports $4\frac{1}{4}''$ long

$2\frac{1}{4}''$

Base $\frac{3}{4}''$